Fathers Are Forever

A Co-Parenting Guide for the 21st Century

Third Edition

STEVEN ASHLEY

ISBN: 0-9740714-1-2

Steven Ashley

www.divorcedfathers.org

steve@divorcedfathers.org

*   *   *

When two people marry and create a child, they make a commitment to care for that child. The majority of the time, they divide the domestic duties and each parent fulfills a different role, either breadwinner or nurturer. When the couple divorces, both parents can still honor their commitment to the child. With the parents no longer living in the same house, however, it makes less sense to divide duties.

When kids spend equal time at both Dad's and Mom's homes, they enjoy two nurturing parents who happily and responsibly participate in their lives. Children who are co-parented have a better chance of growing up with the skills necessary to succeed in life than children of broken families whose fathers are forced to work at every opportunity and forgo parenting.

*   *   *

Dedicated to my father,
Ralph Edward Ashley, 1934-1968
and
To my mother (now), Ruth Levis

CONTENTS

PART I:
THE GOAL OF CO-PARENTING

"It was just foolish of us to think that we could throw someone out of the family and not have everyone suffer."

-Ruth Ashley

CHAPTER 1:
THE FIRST DAYS ARE THE MOST DIFFICULT

As a child, I was very angry with my parents. It seemed my
father had abandoned me. He had been beaten by divorce and
I resented him for not being there. I resented my mom and dad
both for letting the family fall apart.

Mark, a child of divorce

"Nancy moved out," I dutifully wrote in my DAY-AT-A-
GLANCE® book.

It was April 25, 1987. I was imagining Stephany, my two-
year-old, growing up wounded, feeling as I had when my
father left me. In 1968, just nineteen years before, following
the break-up of his marriage, my father chose to end his life.
He left me emotionally scarred and burdened with grief. And
now, after five years together, Nancy, my partner, left with
our daughter. Shocked, I had no plans for the future; not for
Stephany — who I loved most in this world — and not for
myself. So it was in that terrible year I too contemplated
suicide. Fortunately for Stephany and myself, I did not follow
my father to the grave. And, although I shared only fourteen
years of his life, I still think of my dad in a positive way.

Our time together showed me how important a father is to
his child. Even though our home was at times a wild and
tragic place, I still experienced some degree of love, security,
and bonding. Though he took his own life, Dad remained my
hero; no one could take his place. He was the man, after all,
who taught me to walk quietly in the woods and to look
people straight in the eyes when I talked. By his example, he
demonstrated that it was good to work hard and to take pride
in oneself. These simple lessons produced fond memories, yet
the primal connection — the need to have a father — was
deeper still.

Years after his death, I imagined I saw my father in a crowd of people, or driving past in a car, or standing in line at the grocery store. I wanted my mentor, my companion, my best friend — my dad. Even though he was not successful in the usual sense of the word — wealth and power — he did pass on one of life's basic truths: Children need fathers who will maintain a continuing presence in their lives.

What caused my father's downfall was his inability to reach out for help. Instead, he isolated himself and failed to recognize situations where he needed support, such as with his drinking and his crumbling marriage. It would have been far nobler of him to have asked for assistance. However, in spite of his limitations, my experiences with him serve and empower my life today.

Over the past nine years, I have spoken with hundreds of men, many with dads who for one reason or another ceased to be in their lives. Every man admitted he wanted to be loved and needed by his father. North American society has yet to realize how essential fathers are to their children's well-being, and many of us don't recognize that until they are gone.

"I meant to shock your father into getting some help," my mother says today, explaining the circumstances of their break-up. "I was at my wits' end. You see, in the early years, our marriage was a good one. Ed was handsome and witty and lots of fun to be with. As an electrician, he could get a job anywhere... so we traveled. In the 1950s, people who lived as we did were known as 'boomers.' I remember once we even chipped in and bought an abandoned airfield in New Mexico and converted it into a drag strip so Ed could race cars for money. We used to spend our weekends at the airfield fooling around and hanging out with friends. Your dad would race his souped-up Willys coupe against other men's Cadillacs. He won a car or two racing for pink slips. In some ways, your father was like that Willys coupe of his — small and full of surprises.

He would be crossing the finish line before those
Cadillacs got up to speed."

My mom always smiles when she talks about dad and his
fast cars. He enjoyed his freedom and, at the same time,
worked to support the family by moving from one
construction project to another. In the late 1950s, our family
arrived in Santa Cruz. Dad went to work for a local electrical
contractor who was responsible for installing the electrical
system that still powers the University of California at Santa
Cruz.

I have memories of myself as a ten-year-old hiking with
my dad over grassy hills and through the cool redwood forest.
He would point to deer and trees and tell me which college
buildings were going up there. He loved Santa Cruz as it was
at that time — a sleepy retirement community — and, ready to
put down roots and stay in one place, thought it would be a
perfect location to raise a family.

Once the University opened its doors, students swarmed
into town, and Santa Cruz began to change. Again my father
was ready to move on, but my mom, who then held a well-
paying position with the Department of Motor Vehicles,
wanted to stay.

> "My success at DMV was a real ego buster for your
> dad. I used to tell him when we were arguing, before
> we divorced, 'I don't need you, Ed.' You see, I was
> working at a time when most women didn't, and I hired
> baby-sitters when other mothers stayed at home.
>
> "Your dad's drinking got worse. Sometimes he'd play
> football with Randy, Dawn and you... his kids... on
> Saturday morning, and then just disappear until he'd
> turn up again Wednesday."

He drank more and more, possibly to make up for the
painful relationship with his verbally abusive father. I have
heard stories of how my grandfather ridiculed his children in
public and how painful that was for my father. My dad longed

for a loving, supportive family, but his deep-seated hurt and unresolved problems overwhelmed him. He and my mother quarreled frequently. Once he had been a man who took pride in how he looked — strutting out the door and off to work in sharply-creased khakis. As his drinking worsened, he let himself go and became more and more haggard as he lost sight of his dream.

Like other children whose parents divorced, I was both relieved when my mother's and father's fighting ended and at the same time devastated when dad moved out.

Separated from my mother and living alone in a motel room, my dad was served with a restraining order. This occurred just before Christmas. Ignoring the restraining order, he tried to visit his kids, but because he had been drinking, my mother turned him away. As my father left, he grabbed the garden hose and threw it into the back seat of his car. He drove eight miles to Watsonville, and parked behind a little bar called "My Place." With the engine idling, he pushed one end of the hose into the tail pipe and left the other end lying on the back seat. He got back in the car and shut the door. Ralph Edward Ashley died December 26, 1968.

That day, the day after Christmas, I spent hanging out at the beach until it was time to head home. As I walked towards our house on Center Street, I saw my mother standing on the front lawn surrounded by neighbors and friends. She met me with the muscles of her face straining to hide her trembling chin. Her eyes were puffy and red. She struggled to hold herself together.

"Steven, your father has killed himself."

At once defiant and numb, refusing to feel the pain, I asked, "Can I have his car?"

Shocked at my apparent lack of emotion, she gasped, "No! It's full of his blood!"

For months after my father's suicide, I lived in fear of any stressful situation, afraid that I might explode into sobs.

7

Occasionally, the suffering bubbled to the surface. My chin quivered, my eyes filled with tears, and I hid my face from my friends. Some days I just stayed in my room to avoid the risk of further embarrassment. Soon I was trying to escape the pain by drinking beer and smoking marijuana. It didn't work.

Many years later, I realized I couldn't hide from my grief. I felt I had no alternative but to examine my past and deal with the hurt. Once I knew what my parents had been through — and experienced some of that myself — I was no longer the victim. I was free to move on with my life.

Recently, my mother explained the social attitudes at the time she and Dad broke up. "Divorce with co-parenting was not considered. Your father was to visit, I think, one weekend a month. Very few people divorced in those days, and we did not consider any options or the consequences."

It seems few people asked what would happen to the children when one of their parents was removed or, indeed, what would become of the parent who appeared every week or two as a visitor. Then — as now — most people simply followed a system that failed to protect and nurture the needs of all family members.

"Twenty-eight years ago, when I divorced your father, it gave us all this awful sense of failure, and there was no support system, really. Even your best friend is not as good as a family member when you need help. It was just foolish of us to think that we could throw someone out of the family and not have everyone suffer."

Today, looking across the yard at the white front door of the two-story house where my family once lived, I now see how our society, lacking in imagination and understanding, sets mothers and fathers against one another — and causes children to feel shamed and abandoned.

Then as now, children often grow up with ill-informed parents, adults who are ignorant of their options and, therefore, unable to create new models.

As a parent, I understand how difficult it is to make time during a family crisis to look for a better way. The obstacles that work to prevent couples from finding positive new solutions haven't changed. Too often friends and counselors encourage others to follow in their footsteps, even if their paths led to disaster. It takes time and courage to discover something better. In the context of divorce, where the mental health of loved ones, the custody of children, and possession of property are concerned, it is critical that we search for the best alternative. Fortunately, the love for our family is often powerful enough to drive us to do something different, especially when we discover that the solutions of previously divorced parents often created excessive damage and pain.

When a father commits to looking at divorce objectively, and thinks past the divorce decree, he can find positive goals for himself, his ex-wife and their kids. His vision for the future, if built on compassion and understanding, can be the catalyst for the reconstruction of his family.

An Objective View

In a *Time* magazine article, "The Price of a Broken Home," [February 27, 1995], Judith Wallerstein reports the results of studying 131 children whose parents were divorcing:

"Eighteen months after the breakup…we didn't see a single child that was well adjusted. And we didn't see a single child to whom divorce was not the central event of their lives… We realized that the whole trajectory of the child's life changes. Over half of the [now grown] children I have been studying have psychological problems they attribute to divorce."

Judith Wallerstein's conclusions have long been corroborated by more statistically comprehensive studies. Princeton's Sarra McLanahan, a recognized expert in social studies, found that "children of divorce drop out of high school, became teen mothers [and fathers], and are jobless far more frequently than their peers." Experts like Wallerstein and McLanahan bring to our attention some of the by-products of divorce — children unable to succeed in society, and young adults crippled in their attempts at love.

Currently in the United States, according to the Coalition of Parental Support (C.O.P.S.), 18 million children live in single parent households. The following statistics were supplied by C.O.P.S. The first set deals with young women raised in fatherless families:

- 71% of teenage pregnancies are to children of single parents.

- Daughters of single parents are 2.1 times more likely to have children during their teenage years than are daughters from intact families.

- Daughters of single parents are 53% more likely to marry as teenagers.

- Daughters of single parents are 164% more likely to have a premarital birth.

- Daughters of single parents are 92% more likely to choose to opt out of their marriages.

Young men, like their female peers, are at risk when raised in fatherless families:

- 90 % of all homeless and runaway children are from fatherless homes.

- 75 % of all adolescent patients in chemical abuse centers come from fatherless homes.

- 63 % of youth suicides are from fatherless homes.

- 85 % of all youths incarcerated grew up in fatherless homes.

Some parents ask, "If I remarried, would I lower the risk to my children?" Unfortunately, remarrying doesn't offer much protection. Again, according to statistics, seventy-five percent of all second marriages fail.

Today, the percentage of marriages ending in divorce is almost twice that of 1968, the year my parents separated. Using the *Statistical Abstract of the United States*, 1960 through 1994, we can see a progressive disintegration of the family as shown by the increase in divorce and annulment. In 1910, 8.75% of marriages ended in divorce; in 1930, 17.39% unions failed; in 1960, 25.80% of all marriages failed; and in 1990, 48% of those who said they would remain together later changed their minds. In 1992, according to *Time*, 2.3 million couples married and 1.2 million couples divorced. The U.S. Census Bureau currently projects six out of ten first marriages will end in divorce.

Of the more than thirty million couples who have divorced in the last thirty-four years, a few individuals have come up with workable alternatives to the traditional "solution": *The kids go to Mom, and Dad visits.*

No longer is it necessary for single or divorced mothers to miss opportunities to pursue a financially rewarding career. Single men and women do not have to be trapped at home and solely responsible for caring for the kids.

I am grateful for my mother's tenacity and courage, and the fact that she never abandoned her three children. But Randy, Dawn and I watched her struggle daily to provide for us. Typically, she arrived home after working so exhausted that she could only collapse onto the couch.

Today, fathers are still expected to move out of the house and to send money. Society's message is clear: If you continue to work and send a certain amount of money every month you can see your children on the weekend. If you don't, your wages will be attached and, if the problem continues, you will be sent to jail.

Why should dads be forced to spend every spare moment struggling to earn enough money to support two homes — especially when they see the devastating effect their absence has on their children?

There Is a Solution

When two people marry and create a child, they make a commitment to care for that child. The majority of the time, they divide the domestic duties and each parent fulfills a different role, either breadwinner or nurturer. When the couple divorces, both parents can still honor their commitment to the child.

With the parents no longer living in the same house, however, it makes less sense to divide duties. Can we expect Dad to work harder, providing more financially, in return for less time with his child while Mom, also working hard, receives the gift of their children's presence?

When kids spend equal time at both Dad's and Mom's home, they enjoy two nurturing parents who happily and responsibly participate in their lives. Children who are co-parented have a better chance of growing up with the skills necessary to succeed in life than children of broken families whose fathers are forced to work at every opportunity and forgo parenting.

What is co-parenting? It is a proven option, far better than visitation.

Two parents living apart share the responsibility of raising their children and each parent, independent of the other, provides for the children's emotional and physical needs. Both parents are self-supporting and working to be financially independent.

Eloise Anderson, director of California's Department of Social Services, says that she believes fathers can nurture children just like mothers can and that she wants to take some of the financial weight off fathers and place it on mothers. It's an idea whose time has come.

Mickie and Dan know from experience that co-parenting works. They divorced when Deirdre was six and raised their daughter cooperatively until she was twenty-four years old and had graduated from U.C. Santa Barbara with a Masters in Biology. Mickie has this to say:

> "If I would have set out to collect child-support from my daughter's father I would have had to make him my

enemy. He wasn't really. Our marriage was detrimental to all three of us, but our parenting didn't have much wrong with it.

"Co-parenting gives women a chance to get their self-esteem and self-worth from places other than men and our image as mothers. For men, I think it gives them a chance to have their ego satisfaction come from raising their children well instead of competing with the outside world.

Working Together for the Good of All

Another reason both parents must be self-sufficient is they may not have the rapport necessary to work as a team. According to the Kelly and Wallerstein's study, "Surviving the Break-up," fifty percent of mothers see no value in the father's continued contact with the children after separation. Stanford Braver, in the *American Journal of Orthopsychiatry*, 1991, states that 40% of mothers respond that they had interfered with the non-custodial father's visitation on at least one occasion in order to punish the ex-spouse.

Divorced couples should work to lessen the impact of negative change on their families. For the good of all, parents who find themselves incapable of living together now need to provide two independent homes to care for their kids. Doing so will demonstrate to their children that both parents are committed, capable, and loving adults.

A divorced father needs to remain in his children's lives. This is true even if both parents remarry. If a man remarries and his new wife has children of her own, he should not be distracted from his responsibility to his own offspring. From the children's point of view nothing is valued more then their relationship with Dad and nothing hurts more than having their father give his love to a step-child instead of to them. His new wife's children, when old enough to understand, may not respect a disloyal stepfather either.

With women wanting the opportunity to have well-rounded lives, and fathers eager for the opportunity to co-parent, the equal sharing of parental responsibility after divorce is an idea that fits the times. Unfortunately, there are fathers who are afraid to parent, women who do not want to take on financial roles, judges with outmoded ideas, and counselors who view men as inept caregivers for children.

Today, it is the father who can take the lead in a process that moves one broken family into two cooperative homes. His determination to parent more and on an equal footing with his former partner can help his children survive divorce with a minimum of trauma. His insistence on parenting can also benefit the mother by allowing her to do more with her life. Dad can create a win-win situation.

CHAPTER 2: THE MARRIAGE IS OVER

After visiting my children at their mother's house, I have stopped half a block down the road, pulled my car over, and sat there sobbing, feeling my loss again and again.

Tom Alibrandi, Author and Educator

A marital breakup is usually preceded — and followed — by months or even years of bickering and arguing over issues relating to children and the family's finances. In the process, the sanctity of the home is destroyed. A first priority of responsible parents is to do all they can to rebuild, as best they can, what has been torn down. A new home must somehow be built on the foundation of the old in order for the children and the parents themselves to feel secure. There is much to do, and time is critical. As difficult and painful as it may seem, there is a beginning, middle, and ending to the process of reconstructing the family and there is much a devoted father can do to help his children and himself to heal.

Many fathers chose to improve the quality of their lives and the lives of their children by making a commitment to co-parent with their child's mother. Co-parenting provides both mom and dad with an opportunity to work, provide for, and protect their offspring.

However, most men are bitter and hurt following the breakup of their family and are anything but optimistic when someone suggests they adopt a co-parenting arrangement. Ironically, if they would think of their needs, co-parenting makes perfect sense. It allows moms and dads time for parenting, work, and solitude, and the children benefit in every way.

Counselors who oppose co-parenting say that moving children from home to home damages them. Deidre, now a graduate student in biology, was co-parented for fourteen years. In answer to those who question co-parenting, she responds, "For me it would have been horrible to live with only one of them.... They both love being parents and I love both of them."

A well-informed and determined man stands a good chance of rebuilding his family. He and his children may again enjoy a quality life. The following sections explain how to progress from the grief, hurt, and confusion that caring parents feel following a break-up to establishing a workable and healthy co-parenting relationship.

The Right to Parent

Donald T. Saposnek, Ph.D., and Chip Rose, J.D., (Doctor of Jurisprudence) C.F.L.S. (Certified Family Law Specialist), see in divorce litigation a process they call the "negative reconstruction of spousal identity": "This phenomenon is characterized by the tendency of one spouse to cast the other in a vilified image. These intensely negative, polarized characterizations that high-conflict divorcing couples make of each other become reified and immutable over time. The spouse, in essence, rewrites marital history and selectively perceives only the events over the years that fit..."

Frustrated and unhappy in her marriage, Janet was thinking of breaking up with her husband, Jake, a computer programmer. She began keeping a journal with the hope that the objectivity she'd gain in writing about her relationship would help her decide whether or not to remain married. In actuality, she wrote in her journal only when she was upset and, in her view, Jake was always the cause.

Janet began her journal soon after the birth of Linda, their first child. She and Jake acknowledged they had problems. There were discussions about going together to see a counselor, but neither sought outside help. Jake, while he was aware of Janet's ambiguity concerning their marriage, did not know she was keeping a journal.

16

Nine months after Linda was born, Janet quit her job in order to stay home and prepare for the arrival of their second child. Eight months later, Alice was born. Soon after the youngest's arrival, Janet phoned Jake at work and left a voice mail message saying she was leaving him and taking the kids. Jake — in shock — arrived home to discover his children were gone. The furniture had also been removed, the children's possessions were missing, and half of their savings had been drawn out of the bank.

Still reeling, Jake was informed by a sheriff that Janet had sent copies of her journal to the District Attorney's office, to Child Protective Services, and to her attorney. The sheriff told Jake only that Janet had left the state with their children and, while he knew where they were staying, he was not going to give out their location.

A short time later, Janet returned and initiated the divorce process.

Later, reading his wife's journal, Jake felt he had been set up for betrayal. "I couldn't believe what I was reading. Everything was an exaggeration. Yes, there was a thread of truth at times, but nothing happened as she recorded it." For that reason, he was surprised how much weight his wife's journal carried with the authorities.

Jake hired a respected attorney, but she too was influenced by the journal. After investing thousands of dollars, the court order allowed him two hours a week of supervised visitation with his children. His child support payments would be $1,200. a month, slightly over half his net income.

After two years of negotiation with his ex-wife (parent to parent), Jake now sees his children nearly fifty percent of the time. His relationship with Janet is civil and cooperative. They communicate well and share the common duties of providing for their children.

Over the past nine years, attempting to help divorced men, I have listened to hundreds of stories. Almost all divorced fathers have the same concerns:

- How can I reestablish myself as a father and parent my children?

- How can I co-parent with my children's mother when we can't communicate?

- How can I protect myself against a legal system that casts me in the role of "Bad Guy" and demands more money of me than I can earn?

- How do I overcome the fear that I will not be allowed contact with my kids?

- How do I deal with an ex-wife who seems to want total control of the family?

- How do I deal with family law authorities who know little of my former mate or me, yet make decisions that have long-term affects on everyone involved?

There are no laws stating dads must accept a bum deal, yet every day uninformed men settle for less than they need to. Chip Rose, founder of the Mediation Center of Santa Cruz, California, explains it this way:

> "There is rational discrimination. The courts have said, 'if you can show a reason for discrimination, it would be allowed.' An example would be the decade of quotas, 1970-1980, when women and minorities received preferential treatment to counterbalance the previous irrational discrimination against minorities and women. Today in the family law courts, there is a rational discrimination that favors women; (it) flows out of the natural allocations of labors that most couples create themselves. Mom gets pregnant, stops being functional (as a money-earner), stays at home, produces their child, and wants to be there to nurse. Dad is typically full of pride and wants his family

protected so, he happily takes on all the income-earning responsibility."

Co-parenting problems can begin when Mom and Dad decide that only the mother-to-be should have a few months rest before and after a child is born. Often there follows an agreement to let the mother stay home for a few months more to nurse and care for the infant, while Dad continues providing for his family. Many times men begrudgingly agree to continue financially supporting the family well past the time when the mother could have gone back to work. A better option, seldom used by couples, is for both parents to spend equal time at home raising their children.

A history of shared parenting is important. Otherwise, if a break-up occurs, Dad will be expected to continue carrying the income-earning responsibility, whether his children live with him or not. According to Chip Rose: "In 80 percent of the cases in California, custody goes to the mom. And that is flowing from, by and large, patterns couples create. So what the judges see themselves as doing (is) not discriminating against men because they don't necessarily think they're fit, but they see themselves reinforcing the status quo. And there's nothing judges like more than reinforcing the status quo, because it is not a radical thing for them to do."

Legally, fathers and mothers are expected to share the responsibility of raising their kids. Neither parent has the moral or legal right to coerce the other away from their children. Unfortunately, fathers are often forced out of the family. This is especially common in the first year or two after their divorce. In the *Handbook of Financial Planning for Divorce and Separation*, Donald T. Saposnek and Chip Rose explain:

> "The divorce literature generally suggest that in 75 to 90 percent of all contemporary divorces, one spouse wants out of the marriage while the other does not, with women more often [70 % of the time] initiating the divorce. This non-mutuality of the decision to divorce has major implications for the process of divorce. Since the

departing spouse begins the emotional process several years before the spouse that's left, by the time there is a legal filing for divorce, one spouse is ready to proceed at a time when the other may have just found out that there is going to be a physical separation. Thus, the left spouse may only begin the emotional process of divorce on that day, creating a significant discrepancy in their respective stages of the emotional divorce by the time they reach the office of an attorney."

To protect themselves and the children, it is essential that fathers in the throes of divorce do everything they can to make clear their commitment to the family. At the same time, they need to be aware that self-control is often used as a measure of emotional maturity. In word and in deed, the father makes clear that he wants to remain an involved parent.

When Dad is thinking of the kids, he is bound to be happier than when he is anguishing over his former-spouse. Children's antics, demands and questions go far to keep a parent in the here and now. The responsible father makes clear his commitment to his children at the same time he demonstrates self-control. In word and in deed, the father makes clear that he wants to remain an involved parent.

Whatever their grief, men must learn to detach themselves from their children's mother, understanding she is no longer a resource. Any reliance on her only fuels a belief that she is the most capable parent. Fathers struggling for equal rights need to demonstrate that they are as capable as the children's mother.

The first six months following a break-up are the most difficult. Often a man's actions during this emotional time are used as an example of his dedication to his children. Many men who wish to co-parent keep accurate records of the events that followed their separation from their wife. These detailed accounts serve as financial records, proof of their ability to parent, and as a defense against false allegations.

Almost all divorced men go through a period of time

when they experience anger, humiliation, and fear. Most feel unprepared, unprotected, and financially insecure — even suicidal. Men seeking escape from these feelings often overreact.

Those of us who have been through the breakup of a family know how important it is to reach out to people for understanding. However, the last thing single fathers need is to be criticized, labeled, or included in someone's preconceived ideas. A competent, compassionate counselor can be very helpful, as can other fathers who have had experiences similar to those of a new single father.

Self-reliance is an obstacle for many men. Newly divorced fathers should not attempt to rebuild their families alone for two reasons. First, everything done in the early days of divorce greatly influences what happens later, so it is important to get off on the right foot. Second, good choices can save fathers hundreds of hours of struggle and thousands of dollars, time and money that could be spent helping their children and themselves to adjust to shared parenting.

Jim, a 38-year-old electrician, is a father who, after five years, is still in the process of correcting his mistakes. "Things got off to a bad start," he says. "I fell into disfavor with the judge because I was completely ignorant of family law." Jim's attempt to represent himself in his child custody battle failed miserably; his past legal experience was not sufficient to establish a joint-parenting arrangement.

Jim's example doesn't mean that every father needs an attorney. In fact, many judges would rather speak to a parent than an attorney because ultimately the parents raise the children. What Jim's example tells us, then, is that if he had shown the judge that he was a prepared parent — rather than a pseudo attorney — the judge would have been more receptive.

Tom, a co-parent with full physical custody, suggests, "Take charge. Talk to friends or authorities, ask them what to expect. Learn from other fathers what to expect *before* your day in court."

Reaching out to men can be challenging at first. One father said, "I was afraid to reach out because men are supposed to be able to stand on their own two feet." Another remarked, "I had not been taught how to ask for support." Many men who are successfully co-parenting today regularly speak with other fathers. Generally the people who set up co-parenting arrangements and remain involved with their children enjoy helping others do the same. Caring fathers can be a motivational force and can serve as role models to those who are struggling to co-parent.

Greg is a general building contractor in his late thirties who has been raising his daughters in conjunction with his former-wife for the past five years. When she filed for divorce, he grabbed the phone book, looked under *Churches*, phoned, and asked for a counseling pastor. That call provided him with the opportunity to meet people who would help. He walked in to his first church-sponsored Divorce Recovery Group and nervously joked, "Hi, have you got anything for a clueless guy like me?" From that moment on, he says, his life began to change for the better. "I felt I was safe. The people knew how I felt, and they wanted to help."

Four years later, Greg is still using the available resources. He continues to learn the skills necessary to work with his ex-wife so that they can better work together to provide for their children. Recently, Rebecca, their thirteen-year-old daughter, began to drink beer and wine abusively and twice ran away from home. Greg placed his daughter with a counselor and joined a parents' support group. The members walked him through a year of visits with judges and various father-daughter power struggles. Having tested her boundaries and discovered she was still under the protection of her parents and the authority of the law, Rebecca settled back into a peaceful routine. Or, as Greg says, "Today, my daughter is as well-behaved as you would expect a teenager to be."

By phoning counselors in the local community, men can usually find support. There may not be a lot to choose from, so some men start their own support networks by phoning each other on a regular "as needed" or "friendship" basis. The important thing is for single fathers not to isolate and deny themselves the valuable resources that may be just a phone call away.

Feeling Like a Failure

Looking back eight years to the day Nancy left with my daughter, I can still see myself standing dejectedly in the doorway of what used to be Stephany's house, blindly staring across our lawn and rosemary bushes. That had been our home, our slice of paradise.

When the mother moved out and took our child, the emptiness in the home was devastating. My voice became the only one in the house, and my daughter's room grew more depressing with each load of toys that Nancy and Peter, her new boyfriend, hauled out. Fortunately, that time has passed, and today Nancy, Stephany and I again enjoy positive lives.

During difficult times, good friends are priceless. Sharing our sadness with others makes us feel better. Those who care about us can validate our feelings by relating how they too have felt. That lessens our loneliness. Also, sharing with friends allows for insights to surface.

Tom recalls telling his friend Mark, "I'm having the hardest time deciding if it would be better for my kids if they lived with their mother or if I should try for full custody." Tom's dilemma was that he believed that his ex-wife had every right to their children. In his mind, he had already ruled out co-parenting as an option.

The inability of Tom and his ex-wife to cooperate made a formal shared arrangement impossible. Tom went on to discuss his situation with friends. "Hearing men reassure me that I was going to be OK, parenting well, and doing a good job as a father was enabling," he says. "Being told you are doing well as a father is encouraging. It is always great to get support from other men."

The idea that going through a family breakup means one is a failure is nonsense. One father confessed, "I was ashamed when my wife divorced me. All of a sudden, I was no better than all the others whose marriages had failed. My wife chose to leave and I'm a loser."

To this, Judith Goodman, a licensed marriage and family child counselor, responds, "When we're triggered (re-feeling intensely), we need to remember that ninety percent of our feelings are from our past, and only the remaining ten percent have anything to do with what is happening currently." It's painful to feel intense negative feelings and, during divorces, fathers need to balance emotion with intellect. If men can remember that most of what they are feeling stems from past events, then reason can prevail and more dads will survive as parents.

What causes many fathers to feel intense pain is the fear that their children are not going to have "good" homes and in turn receive the care and attention that these men long to provide.

This need not be the case. For example, my daughter's experience is that as a result of her mother and father separating — and not fighting — she has one family and two nurturing homes. In short, she has more love in her life than her mother and I might otherwise have been able to provide.

My daughter has not seen or heard her parents argue in over ten years, and every week she witnesses two adults cooperating in order to provide for her. When Nancy and Peter bought a new home farther away from Stephany's school, Nancy chose to drive the extra twenty minutes, each way, so that her daughter could remain in the same school. She never suggested that Stephany and I change our lives to accommodate her choices. Maturity like that builds respect.

Because her parents cooperate, Stephany also has the opportunity to observe two different lifestyles. Neither fits the "Leave it to Beaver" syndrome. In both homes the adults make sure that homework and chores are completed before it's time to play. At her Mom's house, a ten-acre horse ranch, Stephany rides horses and takes care of dogs, cats, rabbits, chickens, parrots, and other animals. It's a busy place. Family vacations with her Mom consist of camping trips to their mountain property and long rides through the Sierras.

When she is at my house, our leisure time is spent socializing. Stephany will have friends over, or we'll visit them. During the summer, groups of us spend days at the beach. Our recreation also involves travel. When she was two years old, we rode the train from California to Texas to visit her grandmother and granddad. There have been trips to Disneyland, Union Square, Candlestick Park, and Raging Waters. At nine we explored Paris and Ireland, and when she was ten we visited her brother, Gale, in Hawaii. Stephany was thirteen when we visited Australia and New Zealand. Exploring the theaters of London and Paris is next.

Other fathers who find that they can no longer cohabit with their children's mother agree that their children are better off with two homes. One reason they feel this way is that in a traditional family, there is always the opportunity for fathers to fall into the provider role and surrender the nurturing role to the mother. A co-parenting father has to cook dinner, do the laundry, make the bed, read the bedtime story. By its very nature, the living situation gives fathers more opportunities to parent.

It is the father's responsibility to see to it that he has adequate time with his children, and cooperative parenting makes that possible. Toni, a co-parenting mother has noticed: "A lot of fathers become more involved when they are divorced... they're kind of forced into spending time with their kids. Because their partnership with the kid's mother did not work out, they have to look at what kind of relationship they want to have with their kids. If they want to be fathers they have to do a lot of things they probably weren't doing before, like taking time off work to be with the kids. A lot of the time it was Mom who took on that role."

Examining our own family histories can reveal the intimate personal dynamics we ourselves experienced as children. Many men discover they were taught disempowering myths, such as women should take care of children because girls are supposedly more sensitive than boys. Social messages that belittle males fortify the belief that fathers can best contribute to their families by earning money. Myths such as these cause many boys to grow up with low self-esteem, and push them into provider (but not nurturing) roles. Newly divorced men, wrongly believing they are somehow unqualified to nurture their children, often won't go through the struggle necessary to fight for their right to co-parent.

To some degree, parents are responsible for what their children don't learn. Today, most young men are not prepared for shared parenting. With over 50% of today's marriages ending in divorce, it is a mistake not to teach both girls and boys how to be nurturing. Co-parenting fathers and mothers can teach their sons, by example, that boys can grow up to be loving and able parents.

Once a father discovers he either is — or can be — a loving, capable parent, he'll give up the low opinion of himself. When he believes he must parent to be happy, it is going to be almost impossible for him to live any other way. With his new self-awareness, he begins to change, as do his circumstances. Typically, divorced men discover that they want to spend more time with their children.

Co-parenting fathers may feel insecure when they begin spending more time with their children. It is a difficult transition to change their focus from work and money to kids and home economics. If the children's mother did most of the networking with other families, the father may be without the company of other active parents. As his friendship circle increases, his loneliness dissipates. Normally, it doesn't take fathers long to feel secure again. A man parenting with confidence is a pleasure to behold: ask any girl or boy laughing and wrestling with Dad in the park.

Tim Hartnett, himself a devoted father and a licensed marriage family child counselor, puts it this way: "The first decision Dad has to make is that his fathering is vital to the child, and counter the myth that mothers are more important to their children than fathers. Both mother and father have the same amount of humanness, and humanness is what's needed to parent children. A lot of men don't get in as much practice because of the way roles were divided before the divorce, so they feel more distant and less than adequate as parents."

When a father discovers that in order to feel good about himself he must continue as a parent, being restricted to visiting his child every other weekend becomes a humiliating and bitter experience. Often divorced men feel controlled by their ex-wives. In reality the culprit may be an antiquated family law system. After being restricted to *merely* visiting their children many fathers feel manipulated, resentful, and cheated of the opportunity to do what they love — spend time with their children. Criticism and suggestions from a man's ex-wife feel insulting. Paying child support often feels like salt in his wound, adding insult to injury.

Eventually, most fathers who are actively parenting learn to trust their intuition. Marsha Sinetar, author of *Do What You Love, the Money Will Follow*, writes, "Turning our lives around is usually the beginning of maturity since it means correcting choices made unconsciously, without deliberation or thought." Such is the path of many men who realize they must be involved in the parenting of their children.

Keith is the father of two girls, ages seven and two. He survived a divorce that was so violent he had to demand protection from the District Attorney.

"I've learned a lot about myself, about my kids' needs and my past relationship with their mother. Today, I am only responsible for my kids, not their mother. I know what is important to me and what is not acceptable. Definitely I have grown in understanding and hopefully will continue to grow. It's been five years since my divorce, and looking back I've never felt more enlightened or empowered."

Currently, Keith cares for his children every other week.

Our Actions Set the Tone for Our Future

"A father's love is way undervalued: Our society is fairly happy with a man who provides a regular paycheck, but if that man tries to provide love and no paycheck, our society is after his throat," cautions Tim Hartnett, MFCC. Rare indeed is the man or woman who believes that a father's time with his children is more valuable than the time he spends working to provide shelter for those same children.

Performing in a vigilant and self-sufficient way can save fathers a lot of grief. The most human of mistakes, such as arriving late to pick his child up from school, could be used against a man. Being vigilant in maintaining one's right to parent is not being paranoid — it's simply practical. The more fathers pay attention to their actions, the less likely they will be to inadvertently jeopardize their relationship with their children. If fathers become lackadaisical about time spent with their kids — that is, take their opportunity to co-parent for granted — the relationship is at risk. If a father expects his ex-wife to help him care for their children when they are with him, his ex may become resentful and try to become the "exclusive" parent.

Toni has co-parented with two husbands and their children for the past twenty years. She is direct when she speaks of co-parenting and her daughter's relationship with her father:

> "Sheena is going to get some things in her life that other children whose fathers are not available are not going to get. She knows her dad. I mean, when I think about their relationship it brings me to tears. I have a picture of her dad and her going fishing when she was two years old. She is still fishing with her dad. She's learning valuable things from him. She can respect men because her father's a good man, because of that she

28

now has more of an opportunity to pick men that are healthy. And I think that's very cool.

"I believe my daughter deserves to be with her father no matter how I feel. Ideally, philosophically and ethically speaking, I'm going to share custody. Do I always want to? No. If it were not the best thing for my daughter, I would have her all the time, and he would visit every other weekend, or not at all. I want my daughter with me all the time... but I know Sheena needs her father as much as she needs me."

Toni's remarks make clear how important it is for fathers to fulfill their end of the co-parenting bargain. Most mothers value time spent with their children and inattention by the father to his children can make a cooperative ex-wife uncooperative.

Most successful single fathers have learned to discuss plans for changing the amount of time spent with their children, or the lowering of child support, or any situation that alters their position as parents. They use church members, counselors, support groups, or peers as sounding boards because bouncing ideas off others helps them to make the best possible choices.

Using a Counselor

Consulting a Marriage Family Child Counselor (MFCC), especially in the first months after the parents separate, can help a man adjust to divorce. A session every week for the first year can enable men to remain focused on the important issues — learning boundaries, communication techniques, and how to overcome resistance to single parenting.

Justin Sterling, the founder of the Sterling Institute, a national organization that produces relationship workshops for both men and women, says, "Isn't it funny how people will spend hundreds of dollars to tune their car's engine, but few indeed want to invest money in themselves, on their thinking?"

So how does a father find a good counselor? By asking friends and associates, and then "interviewing" a few recommended individuals. Before the first meeting, a father should prepare himself by writing down the questions that are uppermost in his mind. For example:

- Can I afford the fee?

- What day and time can I attend?

- What exactly do I want to get out of this?

- How will I know this person is the one for me?

A man looking for help should not be afraid to ask the prospective counselor questions. For example:

- What are your qualifications?

- What areas are you most successful in?

- How do you feel about men raising children?

- How have you helped fathers walk through divorce?

- What would you do to help me remain involved with my children?

- Can you help me to communicate better with my children and ex-wife?

Judith Goodman suggests that a man who is screening others — in our case, looking for a good counselor — check his gut feeling. If you feel uncomfortable, your body is probably telling you this particular counselor is not the one to work with.

Generally, it is wise for men to use male counselors, but this is not a hard and fast rule. Personally, I hired a woman who I felt was both skilled and unbiased, doing so because I thought Nancy would be more receptive to meeting with a female. Still, many fathers reeling from divorce are emotionally hurt and, for some, time must pass before they will be receptive to a woman's counseling, even though many are capable of helping men. In the days immediately following divorce, using a female therapist may slow the recovery process. Any delay in a man's recovery makes setting up a co-parenting arrangement more difficult.

Look for counselors who have a track record of helping fathers remain involved with their children. Many such individuals teach the skills that help families remain involved with each other and understand the bias co-parenting fathers face in our present-day society.

Child Counseling

Immediately after Nancy moved out, I was seeing my daughter for an hour or two, two or three days a week. Stephany's mother was not taking legal action to prevent me from seeing my daughter and, in fact, encouraged the visits. She had, however, taken possession of Stephany and that gave her the ability to control when and where I could see my child. What was bothersome to me was that Nancy seemed to have little interest in protecting my rights as her daughter's father and she was not taking action to create a co-parenting agreement.

At that time I was very confused. I wanted to spend more time with my daughter but I needed to know that my plan to eventually co-parent half time was best for Stephany. There were many questions that needed to be answered. Should I be spending more time with Stephany now? Did she suffer as I did after a visit? What kind of visitation worked for a child two years of age and how would the schedule change as she grew? What did Stephany think of her father all of a sudden becoming a visitor? I decided to hire a professional. I thought Nancy and I needed an education in child development. Maybe a child psychologist would inform Nancy that Stephany needed her father as much as her mother and that a fifty/fifty parenting arrangement was preferable. It was worth a try.

I hired Elizabeth Tatum, a child psychologist, with an office in Nancy's neighborhood. Nancy was willing to listen. I was hopeful that Elizabeth could show Nancy and I how to help Stephany adjust and that her training would support my idea of co-parenting. Early on it was obvious that Ms. Tatum was a good choice — she had my daughter's interest in mind.

In the first session, Elizabeth told me to "get off the cross because we need the wood." After the initial shock wore off, and after a moment's reflection, I saw that I was sounding like a victim. Elizabeth explained that children do not feel sorry for, respect, or reward parents for "playing the martyr." Doing so, she said, only embarrasses them.

Elizabeth Tatum helped educate Nancy and me about parenting and she supported the idea of both parents being equally involved in raising our child. She outlined a parenting plan where my time with my daughter increased as Stephany aged. Nancy was able to accept Elizabeth's co-parenting schedule because — I think — she trusted her training, her experience, and her desire to do what was best for our daughter.

Hiring a counselor as preventative medicine demonstrates to all involved that Dad cares. Therapists are a resource worth using, even though they may, at times, make us uncomfortable.

Claudia, a MFCC who specializes in working with children, became Stephany's counselor later on. She has proven to be an ideal person for my daughter to talk with. A mature woman in her fifties, Claudia has the kindness, honesty, and directness I associate with the classic grandmother.

When Stephany was upset and I suspected there was a problem, Claudia quietly researched the situation in a manner in which I was not qualified. She put Stephany's mind at ease and reassured me that my daughter's concerns were a "natural part of growing up." I thanked Claudia for quieting Stephany's fears and helping both of us to feel secure.

Because counselors are removed from the family, they are less intimidating to children than their parents. Their being outside the family allows children the space to talk about issues that are too difficult, embarrassing, or frightening to share with Mom and Dad. And that can be a godsend for parent and child.

Joel and his former-wife have been divorced for four years. Recently he and Mary were engaged in a power struggle. Joel wanted her to deliver the children to his house after their stay with their mom, and Mary wanted him to pick the girls up. Trying to get what she wanted, Mary told all three daughters to phone their father and ask when he was going to pick them up. Joel was furious. Initially he refused to drive over and get them, but after talking the situation over with another father, he decided to go get his kids. What bothered Joel was that he did not want his ex to use the girls as pawns in their arguments. For that reason he decided to ask the school counselor if she would encourage the girls to ask their mother to speak directly with Dad. Sharing his concern, the counselor agreed to meet with the girls.

Joel says "Mary is still giving the kids messages to give to me — you know, placing them in the middle — but at least now the girls know that it isn't right. Sometimes they'll tell their mom they don't want to tell me what she's said and that she needs to tell me herself. It's pretty amazing."

The counselor we hire can become a special friend to our child; this is good, but there are limits. Children need to know early on that the counselor's only purpose is to help them solve problems. Making sure the child understands that when the problems are solved the visits will end keeps everything in perspective. Without this understanding, children may come to believe that counselors are friends who will always be available.

A professional will maintain the proper client-to-counselor boundary. He or she will keep in mind the financial cost to the parents and will not abuse a parent's trust. It is appropriate, by the way, for a father to ask what issues his child is working on. Bear in mind, too, that if fathers have any doubts about the professionalism of the counselor, they have every right to remove their child.

There may be times when a father needs a counselor's opinion — for example, if a father suspects child abuse has occurred. In this situation, it would be wise to get a professional's opinion as soon as possible. If such fears prove to be grounded in reality, and a crime has been committed, it will be helpful to have an expert on the child's side when it's time to take the suspected abuser to court. If the problem turns out to be a false alarm, the father will at least have thoroughly researched the situation. Then, having responded to a suspected threat to his child, father and child can rest at ease, feeling secure again.

Teaching children to use a counselor gives them the ability to seek qualified help in later years, should they need it.

Children Know What Is Going On

Stephany and I were walking to my truck on our way home, discussing the days' events at school, when she told me about a conversation she had with a friend whose parents were divorcing.

"Kaylan thinks it's all her fault her parents are fighting. She says they fight every time one of them comes to get her. She feels really bad. I told her about Claudia and said Kaylan should ask her dad if she could see Claudia, too."

While sorry to hear that Kaylan was negatively affected by her parents' bickering, at the same time I was struck by the fact my daughter had the resources and willingness to offer help to a friend.

Even children whose parents don't fight in front of them are still strongly affected by separation and divorce. For instance, when parents are grieving, their emotions are impossible to hide from their children.

"Kids always know how their parents feel," says Claudia Alonzo, MFCC, "but unfortunately, in knowing everything, they also, because of how kids think, assume they caused it — they made the situation or feeling happen. I think it just goes with the way a child looks at the world and the universe — they're the center of the universe — that's how children think. That's developmentally what children ought to be thinking when they're little. When parents are having a difficult time, their kids just automatically jump to the conclusion that they caused the problem."

Therefore, not only are we wasting our time when we lie to kids but, by not assuming responsibility for our actions, we allow children to assume guilt that is not theirs.

In the long run, we protect our children by being honest about our feelings — so long as we're careful not to burden them with our emotions. Children need to be excluded from their parents' drama as much as possible.

I was driving my daughter to school one morning and was deep in thought, and feeling sad about our family breaking up, when Stephany asked, "Daddy, why are you sad?" I almost burst into tears. Instead, I used the opportunity to tell Stephany I was sad because her mother and I were unable to live together happily, even though we had tried really hard to do so. By sharing my thoughts with my daughter, I was able to validate her feelings, assume responsibility for our situation, and hopefully prevent her from feeling responsible. When children ask questions, it should be considered validation for capable parents.

Most counselors will say that children ask difficult questions only when they feel safe. Most of the fathers I work with are not afraid to show their emotions to their children — they believe it is healthy to do so — and most know how important it is to maintain self-control. This means as fathers we may cry, but we don't emotionally fall apart. Some children feel insecure when their parents are sad and when that happens, fathers simply remind them that dads take care of kids even when they are sad.

Generally, children learn from their parents' actions. Listening and talking with them, giving hugs or verbal validation, and telling our children we love them — daily —

does more to make them feel secure than anything else we might do. Gifts bought are quickly forgotten, but the intimate moments shared by a father and his child will be long remembered.

On May 30, 1988, I wrote in my journal, "Stephany awoke during the night crying — four times. The torment of her parents' separation is showing itself in bad dreams. It has become very important to her that I read at bedtime until she falls asleep." Not only was this comforting to Stephany, but it soon became extremely important to me. Ten years later we still read every evening we are together. Reading to Stephany is one of the most cherished things we do together.

During those painful days, when Stephany was small and the separation was new, there was a game we played that entertained her and reminded her she was loved. I'd say, "Stephany, do you know how much I love you?" as I opened my thumb and first finger an inch, as if measuring something small. I'd tell her, "More than this much." Then I'd open my thumb and finger wider and say, "More than this much, too." Then I'd open my thumb and finger as far as I could and tell her again, "More than that, too." Then I'd use my hands, and acting as if I were measuring something a foot long, I'd say, "No, more than that much, too." I would continue until my arms were opened as wide as possible, and with a booming voice I'd say, "Stephany, I love you even more than this much... I love you more than I could ever tell you. Do you know that? As a matter of fact, you're my favorite kid in the whole world." We both liked that game and I was sad when she outgrew it.

The point is that kids need to know their fathers love them and will always be there. Who wants to be the father of the child who, now grown, can't remember ever hearing Dad say, "I love you?"

Explaining the Separation to Our Children

Explaining to children why Mom and Dad will no longer live together is very difficult and painful to all concerned. It is frightening because our children mean so much to us. The last thing we want to do is hurt or frighten our kids, and breaking the news to them does both. They need and deserve an explanation, and they have a right to know what to expect in their future. Fathers need to prepare themselves in order to explain the situation properly.

Taking the time necessary to understand what should and should not be said, and then rehearsing, will eliminate a lot of grief. To get a better understanding of what to say, a man can pay for an hour of a counselor's time, or speak with a capable father who has himself been through the process.

Once a father knows what to say and how to say it, he needs to think about the proper place to communicate with his children. The privacy of home usually makes the most sense. Within the home, neutral places such as the living room, the kitchen table, or the back porch work well. These locations provide privacy and are non-threatening. Ensure that there is privacy so everyone can feel safe to express their emotions.

Many fathers ask, "How much explaining should I do?" Depending on their age, children need only to hear those details that are appropriate and directly affect their lives. Children can be damaged by hearing the "gory" details of their parents' lives. Every talk will be different, but an explanation — albeit overly simplistic — might sound something like this:

> "We need to have a family talk. I'll talk first, and then it will be your turn. You know that your mother and I haven't been getting along... so we have decided it is best to get a divorce. This only means that she and I won't be living together. We still love you and both of us are always going to take care of you. We tried as hard as we could to live together and to be happy, but we can't. So in the future you will have two homes: one at this house and one at your Mom's.

> "Your mother and I are separating because we think it is best for all of us. I'll do whatever it takes to help us

get through this. I want you to know that I love you and that I will always be here."

At this point in the conversation, give the children a chance to express themselves, indicating that it is safe for them to vent their feelings, whatever they are. Some may show their pain as anger, others may cry, and still others may show no emotion at all.

Fathers can be certain their children are hurt. Ask them how they feel, hold them if they will let you. Let children know it's okay to cry or to say whatever is on their minds. At this time — especially at this moment — they need to know they matter. Taking the time to prepare, explaining appropriately in a safe place, and then listening assures them that you care.

Kids do not benefit from hearing one parent blame the other. Child counselor Claudia Alonzo says:

> "I don't think any parent should **ever** badmouth the other parent. And that is probably the hardest thing for parents not to do when they split up. Don't give dirty looks, roll your eyes, or look disgusted when the other person's name is mentioned. Those things come back to haunt you, because the child, then, feels the need to defend the parent who's being dumped on. Also, the kid will look at the fact that if one parent thinks the other parent is the scum of the earth, then that means half of the child is the scum of the earth, too, and that doesn't feel very good."

Children will draw their own conclusions. Because of their inexperience, they lack understanding. Seldom will children consider how difficult divorce is for their parents — at times children may seem insensitive.

Bear in mind, no matter how the talk appears to be received, the family will have many painful feelings to deal with. Remember to hold your tongue when tempted to say something negative about your ex-spouse. This will limit conflict, help salve old wounds, and reassure the children that both parents will remain in the "family." This is a key step in preparing for the long reconstruction period during which acceptance and healing must take place.

CHAPTER 3: ESTABLISHING PRIORITIES AND PLANING FOR THE FUTURE

One of the most powerful moments in my life happened when I was ten years old. I was upset about some childhood hurt, I can't remember exactly what today, but I was inconsolable, sobbing my heart out. My dad was sitting on my bed patting my back. He sat there for hours and hours. He didn't leave until I felt better. That was really special... and not unusual. My dad was the more affectionate of my parents. He was the one who gave us our hugs.

Claudia Alonzo

As children, we love our fathers. There's a heart connection that is more than the result of deeds done. It's primal, established during our infancy. The relationship can be seen in the playfulness children display while holding dad's hand when walking, and the laughter caused by being tossed into the air and playfully caught time and time again, and in the blissful face of a infant safely sleeping in dad's strong arms. Even children who have had negative experiences report that under their hurt is the desire to have a loving father.

There are many stories illuminating a father's love for his child. One of my favorites has to do with my daughter and I riding out the aftershocks of the 1989 Loma Prieta Earthquake, drinking root beer floats. Stephany and I lived eight miles from the epicenter. After the initial tremors finished throwing us around, I picked Stephany up and carried her to the safety of our apple orchard. Hoping to quiet her fears, I said, "Stephany how about a root beer float?" I knew if I could put a float together, she would realize we were going to be okay.

The house was in shambles — the chimney was lying on its side in our backyard, the refrigerator stood in the dining area, and our TV was upside down on the living room floor. In between aftershocks, I ran into our house gathering glasses, ice cream, and root beer. Ten minutes later, Stephany and I sat under one of the younger apple trees and drank root beer and ate vanilla ice cream. For the next two days, we camped there and waited for the earth to stop shaking. Every parent has experiences that he or she could cite illustrating their devotion to their children.

A father's life can be both glorious and challenging. What man has not looked in on his sleeping child and not been overwhelmed with gratitude for the opportunity to witness such beauty and innocence? And on the other hand, who hasn't thought, "I can't stand one more minute with that crying child?"

So why does everything change when parents split up? Why do some dads, when they separate from their mates, find it so difficult to remain involved?

More men would co-parent if it were not for obstacles such as:

- Overly possessive mothers

- Antiquated social myths

- Lack of community support

- Judges who frown on co-parenting arrangements

These obstacles test even the most dedicated fathers.

Typically, during custody battles, fathers fight for children they seldom see. When they do visit their sons or daughters, the opportunity is often tainted by conflicts with their children's mother. As the custody and financial battles continue, the animosity escalates. Eventually some fathers say, "The hell with her. I'll give her the kids and see how she likes it." or "This is too much. I can't take any more of this hassle. I'm out of here." Conflict between former mates interferes with the father-child bond; it would do the same to mothers if fathers were awarded custody in the majority of cases.

The fighting can become so intense that parents take the law into their own hands. For example, Americans often receive in the mail missing persons cards requesting information on runaway parents and abducted children. Statistically, mothers and fathers are equally guilty of stealing children.

The legal process necessary to create co-parenting can become so lengthy and painful that some fathers give up the fight for their children. Fathers can use the following questions to keep them focused on their child's needs and to learn more of what motivates men like themselves to parent:

- How important was my dad to me?

- Can I be happy without my child in my life?

- What will my kids think of me if I quit parenting?

- What kind of relationship do I want to have with my children?

- What could I do in my life that would be as rewarding as raising my kids?

For many men, answering questions like these make the idea of walking away from parenting absurd.

Even separated, moms and dads typically want to remain parents. Both want their children to know that they are loved, and both want the opportunity to demonstrate that love.

For children to have nurturing relationships with their divorced parents, fathers have to do their part to create a co-parenting relationship with the mother. Having the mother control the time that he and his child spend together sabotages the mother-father relationship, and in turn hurts the child. Children must witness a balance of power in order to respect both parents. Equality between mom and dad allows children to feel secure and, in addition, teaches them how to co-exist with their mates in the future.

In the midst of divorce, the family situation is fluid. Nothing is permanent. Parenting roles can be changed. Fathers who understand themselves and the affect they have on their children are often empowered by that knowledge to take constructive action. John, a building inspector, went through a difficult process and reached the follow conclusion: "Sometimes I think it would be easier not to fight with my ex. But I can't do that. I mean, I've waited six months for her to let me see my kids. I haven't seem them yet, and she won't tell me when I can. Now I'm going to exercise my options. My kids need to know I love them. I think that matters to them — it sure matters to me. I'm going to let them know I care even if I have to go through the legal system to do it."

Disneyland Dad to Super Dad

Here's what it is like for Cathy, whose ex-husband is a weekend father:

"Nathan's father has remained consistently involved with his son for the five years we have been divorced. I respect him for that. Our son is eight years old. He visits his father for dinner every Wednesday and stays with him every other weekend, which is great. But when he comes home from his dad's house on Sunday nights, he's exhausted and over stimulated. It's from lack of discipline and staying up late with Disneyland dad. Nathan comes home insecure. Sometimes he cries himself to sleep. I think he's still afraid one of us is going to leave again."

With longer visits, Nathan's father probably would feel less of a need to entertain his son. For example, having his kid every other week means Nathan would see his father coping with mundane matters like homework, laundry, and bedtime stories. His dad could model life as he actually lives it. And, Cathy would no longer be handed a child to mend. For Nathan, time spent with Mom would no longer be less entertaining than time spend with Dad.

Further, because young children have a limited comprehension of time, it is hard on them when their father visits every other weekend. If youngsters see their dads every seven or twelve days — which to them appears to be a random visit — they can't understand that a routine is in place. To a toddler, Dad is simply gone, out of the family.

When my daughter was three years old, I established the right to care for her half of each week, from Sunday 8:00 AM through to Wednesday at 5:00 PM. When she asked, "How long can I stay with you, Daddy?" or "When will I see Mommy again?" it was easy to explain. She understood when I responded. "The day after tomorrow," and we counted three fingers. The fact that she was at her mother's and my house the same amount of time each week helped Stephany understand there was a routine, and in turn to feel secure.

Planning to Co-Parent

The father who is determined to share in the parenting should plan how to accomplish his goal. It is essential that he know what is legally acceptable in his county and how the fathers who are co-parenting manage to do so.

Understanding that co-parenting is a difficult transition for the family is the first step towards cooperative parenting. The second step is learning what the possible options are — there are various shared parenting schedules. The third step is to test the feasibility of a plan by noting its benefits to family members.

What follows are some tried-and-true parenting arrangements:

- Fathers are responsible for the kids from Friday after school until they drop them off at school Monday morning. Mom is responsible for them from that moment on until she drops them off again Friday morning.

- Fathers and mothers share parenting every three-and-one-half days, beginning and ending Saturday afternoon.

- Fathers and mothers care for their children every other week, usually beginning and ending on Sunday evenings.

- Fathers and mothers divide parenting by the school year, with one parent looking after the children during the academic year, and the other during the summer.

The imagination seems to be the only limit to parenting arrangements. Unfortunately, some of the more creative schedules, the ones with many child transfers, are difficult for children. But even numerous transfers are not as painful as losing contact with Mom or Dad.

Below is a simple technique to help fathers come up with a co-parenting schedule:

Step 1. Write or explain to someone your desires or plans pertaining to parenting. The idea here is to run your thoughts past an impartial listener in order to clarify them in your own mind.

Step 2. Write or tell someone what your life might look like if you got the parenting arrangement you wanted.

Step 3. List the benefits and losses for every person involved. Do this to further clarify ideas, and to show a well-thought-out plan to your ex-partner or whoever may need to know.

Change Creates Opportunity

Fortunately, parenting agreements are not carved in stone. Greg R. is a carpenter/builder and the father of two girls. He originally found help in his church's single parents group and his co-parenting has evolved to this: "For the last three or four years, I've been a part-time dad and a part-time contractor, because work has been slow. And it's been perfect because it's afforded me the time to go on field trips with my kids, to attend school meetings, and to spend more casual time with them. I've discovered if I don't make time for my kids, none of the rest of my life flows. So, I'm learning about priorities and prioritizing my life."

Many fathers choose to get more involved after they learn how much their children need them. Counselor Tim Hartnett believes fathers are critical to their children's development:

> "Careers, relationships and family are the biggest sources of satisfaction in our lives, and fathers play a major role in these areas. Having a close relationship with one's father can increase a child's chances of

having a satisfying career. Some children internalize their father's confidence in the work place. A daughter may have a close relationship with her father and he may be successful in his career. If she internalizes that, she may develop a sense of personal empowerment pertaining to money — she may be very successful — and that can be a basis of happiness for her.

"Many women have difficulty having relationships with men. If a child comes from a family where there is bitterness from divorce, the mother may have negative attitudes about men in general and Dad in particular. The father needs to be present to show his daughter exactly who he is.

"When girls have a strong sense that men will love them for reasons other than their sexuality — and that is what their dads can provide — then girls stand a better chance of avoiding dysfunctional, over-sexualized relationships. If Dad says, 'I love you because you are my daughter, because of who you are,' when his girl is approached by a guy who only wants sex she may pass the guy by and keep looking for what she knows is possible — a man who loves her for who she is."

Attitudes and Affirmations

For eight years, Tom C., a surveyor in San Jose, California, has had primary custody of his kids, Ryan and Sara.

"My children are the most important part of my life. I believe they will always be. I tell men to think about what is best for their kids and everything will fall into place. What I receive is a far richer life by focusing on my kids. Now I find myself doing things that I wouldn't have done earlier. For example, I wouldn't have participated in Little League. I wouldn't have gone to their school and worked with them on activities. I wouldn't have had the laughs I got watching my kids perform in plays. All of which I view as a gift."

The determination to parent is crucial. I have never known a father to fail who was willing to meet every obstacle placed in his path.

Greg R. sums up his commitment this way: "I'll remain a player. Looking back, I have been onboard, co-parenting, for five years now. I feel really good about that… about myself and my life… and believe me, it hasn't been easy."

Francis Farley, 1993-1996 World Champion kick boxer, gives this advice about the mental preparation necessary to overcome challenges. The youngest of four brothers, Francis has faced and overcome many battles. "Most contests are won or lost before anyone enters the ring. The person who believes in himself almost always wins. To beat a person with an advantage, you have do your road work, and then you have to believe in yourself more than your opponent believes in himself. The person who does that consistently gets to be the world champion."

Affirmations for Maintaining Focus

- My children are a gift and no one has the right to stand between them and me.
- I am a capable parent and I enjoy being with my children.
- I teach my kids what I know and am there for them when they need me.
- The time I spend with my children benefits them more than the money I earn working.

Mentally repeating statements like these can help men to succeed in custody battles.

Today, Greg R., once an angry, disempowered father, now facilitates divorce recovery groups in the church where he himself sought help. His advice: "Open up, be vulnerable, let people know who you are, and what is going on. Five years ago, I told the people at the church's Divorce Recovery Group that it was difficult being a single father. They cared. Today, if a man wants to parent, help is available in most communities. Support and training has made a huge difference in my life."

Like most children, my daughter went through a great deal of pain following my separation from her mother. Tears in her eyes, Stephany would say, "I want my Mommy... why won't you and Mommy live together anymore?" I would be fighting back tears. Then I'd question myself: Am I somehow compelling — forcing — my daughter to stay with me against her will? Am I being selfish in my desire to continue parenting? Have I taken on too much? The transition to co-parenting is harder than I thought it would be. Maybe I should just give in and drive Stephany back to her mother's.

The bottom line is that our relationship was too good to surrender. I knew Stephany loved me as much as she loved her mother and I understood what was best for her was to have *both* parents remain in her life.

As painful as it was to see her crying, I had to trust my beliefs and go with co-parenting. Giving in to her crying would have conveyed the message that Stephany could control her parents by displays of emotion. In time, she would have lost faith in her parents and become increasingly insecure. In the long run, the only way a child can feel secure is if both parents adhere to a schedule and remain adults. How else will children become used to a new parenting arrangement?

Fortunately, I spoke with other parents and an experienced counselor. Elizabeth Tatum, a child psychologist, told Nancy and me that children ask for the other parent until they realize neither Mom nor Dad is going to abandon them. She reminded us that divorce is *the* major upset for children.

Children, as well as parents, need time to adapt to a whole new living arrangement. A few weeks later, while talking with Nancy about Stephany's state of mind, Nancy was able to share with me that Stephany had been asking for me, too. I felt better — reassured that I, too, would be playing a major role in Stephany's development.

Sadly, I know men who have given up their children during emotionally difficult times. They were mistaken when they thought it was the noble thing to do.

CHAPTER 4: COMMUNICATION SKILLS

- When communication is stressful, discuss only the important stuff.
- Think about your former partner positively before a difficult talk.
- Don't show your hand or offer too much information.
- Watch out for buttons and triggers, hers and yours.
- Use humor whenever possible.

Tips for Surviving the First Year
(Divorced Fathers Network, Santa Cruz, CA, 1/10/2000, group brainstorming session)

Expressing himself well does not guarantee a man's right to remain a parent; however, constructive dialogue can minimize the stress, time and money necessary to build a co-parenting relationship. More and more, fathers are ending the adversarial divorce process by convincing the ex-wife, the child custody counselor, and the judge that the wellbeing of the couple's children hinges on the father being allowed to co-parent.

For many couples in the divorce process, their desire to communicate is at an all-time low. The ability they once had to cooperate may be gone, replaced by self-defeating bickering. If a parent decides that through divorce she or he can take control of the children, the home, and child support, winning at all costs will take precedence over communication.

One of the tragedies of divorce is that it interferes with the parents' will and need to communicate. For many divorcing couples, children, money, and property become trophies or prizes to be won and guarded.

It is at the very time that Mom and Dad are separating that their children most need them to cooperate. Parents who communicate with one another are more able to give their children what they need: emotional support and physical security.

When dealing with an ex-spouse seeking sole physical custody of the children--and counselors and judges who may favor that scenario — a father must learn to communicate very well indeed if he hopes to enlist their cooperation.

A man has to be able to present his ideas well enough to convince his audience that his proposal has merit. That should open the door to mediation and increase the chances of the parents negotiating a workable arrangement. Occasionally men will encounter individuals who say, "I don't think bouncing children from house to house is a good idea." When that occurs, a father will have to explain how the benefits to the children of such an arrangement outweigh the inconvenience. Dads might also point out that studies show that children who have regular and continued contact with both parents benefit throughout their lives. In short, it is Dad's job to look out for the needs of the children, and that includes regular continued contact with both parents. Children need both parents more than they need a single residence to call home.

Faulty Logic — Objections to Co-Parenting

Still, some mothers, counselors, and judges will favor parenting plans that, in essence, separate children from their devoted fathers. Many of these so-called experts operate out of the belief that parents who can't communicate should not share in the raising of their children. John DeWit (not his real name), a court-appointed mediator assigned to Tom Martin, remarked after the first mediation session, "I hesitate to write up a fifty-fifty parenting schedule. In the 1980s it was tried and it didn't work out. Too many parents continued to argue."

Tom responded, "This mediation proceeding isn't setting the stage for cooperation. Why would my ex-wife negotiate with me knowing you feel that way?"

It is common for Family Law Courts to employ "experts" to make parenting recommendations to judges. Many of these court employees have themselves gone through contentious divorces with lengthy custody battles. The percentage of divorced custody counselors, emergency screeners, Assistant District Attorneys, and county-employed family law mediators appears to me to be greater than the national average for divorce.

Most are single mothers and too few have personal experience as co-parents. Based on their own experiences, some conclude that co-parenting is unattainable for the average untrained divorced parent. For many of the family law experts, especially those who were unable to make co-parenting work in their own lives, cooperative shared parenting is an unpopular idea. Like John DeWit, they mistakenly believe the way to limit hostility between ex-partners is to limit the child's time with one of the parents. There are three problems with this logic:

1.   The parent with less contact feels short-changed. Feeling cheated fuels resentment and perpetuates conflict.

2.   The parent assigned less time with his or her children usually strives to gain more parenting time. Fighting for the child's company places the child in the center of the conflict, which supports the child's belief that he/she somehow caused the problems.

3.   Too many judges, counselors, and parents forget that separating a child from either parent damages both the child and the alienated parent. There is evidence that children emotionally harmed in custody battles become problems the community must later incarcerate or treat. (See the statistics in Chapter 1.)

Even in extreme cases, where one parent can't be civil in the presence of the other, co-parenting can still work. Using the available resources and living in separate homes, both parents can still be providers. If necessary, they can use a third person as a "go-between" when exchanging children or messages. Since sharing custody limits child support, co-parenting removes one more possible irritant.

After co-parenting without contact for a couple of years, even the most vengeful parents can develop a respect for the other's devotion to the child they have in common and whose well-being depends on them both. In time, divorced individuals even become grateful for the other's support, but it is often a long time before that is felt and expressed.

Stressing the Benefits of Co-Parenting

The most influential communication for fathers starts with honesty. Statements like "I want to care for my children because I love them and they need me" are hard to contest. However, when a man expresses his love for his children he has to understand that cynics may label him co-dependent. Jim B., the father of a toddler, became tearful while pleading for an extra evening a week with his daughter. The judge overseeing Jim's case responded by saying, "You're co-dependent. You're spending too much time worrying about your child and this case. Why don't you put more of your energy into work?"

When Jim was expressing his desire to parent, he leaned heavily on emotionalism. He may have done better if he had remained level-headed and stressed the benefits to the child of having two involved parents.

Sad, but true: In our present-day society, men must toe the line and not allow their feelings as loving parents to be misconstrued or labeled "obsessive."

In the context of co-parenting, communication is the most important of all skills. A father can't afford to be arrogant. It will be difficult for even the most skilled communicators to promote co-parenting to an ex-wife or counselor who opposes the idea. The rewards of thoughtful communication include peace of mind and better relationships with those around us.

Strategies for Success

What can a father do to improve communication with counselors, judges and ex-spouses?

- Show up for appointments on time and pay attention. Listen intently and, as appropriate, repeat back in your own words what you heard him/her say. Remember to ask if what you heard was what the speaker wanted to communicate.

- Make eye contact and show you're listening. Be sure your body language is non-aggressive.

- Put yourself in the position of the other person and try to see the situation from their point of view.

- Use "I" statements to explain what is important to you and avoid blaming the other party. For example, "I'd like to spend more time with the children — I feel it's important to them. I also think when both parents have equal time with the children there will be less reason for conflict."

- Talk things over with another father — preferably someone who is himself engaged in co-parenting — before speaking with counselors, judges or the children's mother. Ask the other father if you sounded angry or blaming. Practice until you can communicate in an assertive, yet non-threatening manner.

- Say only what is necessary — too much input can confuse the issue.

- Maintain self-control. Sharing children with someone who wants no part of you, or who you want no contact with, requires self-discipline. The better you can communicate, the easier it will be for all those involved.

When parents first separate they often feel angry and defensive. Trust is at an all-time low. There may be a tendency to imagine the worst. One way to short circuit real or imagined fears is to present all the details that are relevant to the communication at hand.

John Grinder, a communications consultant, offered some suggestions to men attending a Divorced Father's Network Meeting. *Framing*, he suggested, is a way to give one's former spouse the details and, in turn, the opportunity to fully understand what is being stated or requested.

When she sees the whole picture, she has a better chance of accepting the logic behind any given proposal and the benefits to her.

Framing is the art of first presenting the details that surround one's point or suggestion before discussing the subject itself. Generally, fathers frame statements and questions in order to facilitate cooperation. When a suggestion or idea is well framed it is easier for the other person(s) to understand and encourages their participation.

Here is an example:

Instead of arbitrarily saying to an ex-partner, "I'm picking the kids up early on Saturday morning," try framing. "I've been thinking that it would be good for the kids to see more of nature. I would like to take them to the zoo. The only time I could get tickets for the guided tour was at 9:00 a.m., so I'd like to pick the kids up an hour early on Saturday morning, about 8:00. What do you think?"

Now the mother knows why the father wants to pick the kids up early. If she is able to place her children's well-being before any negative feelings she may have for him, and she too feels the kids will benefit from the field trip, the father will pick his children up an hour early on Saturday morning.

A father who was scheduled for custody mediation in seven days set out to master framing. From one Monday to the next, he made a conscious effort to frame every question and statement so it was complete, logical and appealing.

He mastered the fine line between saying too much, and appearing manipulative, and saying too little and leaving out essential details. His mediation went well: he received more time with his children than he expected. An unforeseen benefit was the kudos he received from his ex-wife who appreciated the extra details as well as the man's effort to better communicate.

Asking questions is essential to good communication. Asking questions allows one to understand exactly what someone else is saying. Often what is heard is not what the speaker intended to communicate. Questions are used to explore what has been said. There are two types that are equally important for good communication:

First are the questions that explore the *consequence*s of what is being presented. For example, one's ex-wife might say, "You are feeding the kids too much junk food."

Instead of responding defensively: "No I'm not, and stop telling me what to do," a father could pause, take a deep breath and ask, "What happens when I give the kids junk food?"

The mother then has the opportunity to explain the consequences she is trying to avoid. Her explanation could be: "They are so sugared-out after they visit you that they don't fall asleep until after midnight, and their schoolwork suffers because I have to send them to school tired."

People are surprised at how often exploring the consequences of the subject at hand leads to a better understanding and, in turn, works to the benefit of both parents and children. An added benefit is that a full disclosure allows the mother to feel heard and, as a result, more willing to communicate with you. In such instances, questioning can lead to a better co-parenting relationship — the father more thoroughly understands the problem and the mother is pleased by his willingness to get to the core of their issues.

Sometimes, though, an ex-spouse's answer will make absolutely no sense. When that happens, a father can simply say, "I'm sorry. I'm not sure I understand," and instead request, "Can you clarify... can you tell me more about your concerns?"

Questions are also helpful when wanting to explore a generalization. Accepting a broad statement, especially if it is accusatory, often means a missed opportunity to research the issue at hand. For example:

If an ex-wife were to say, "Joe, you don't know how to take care of little children," Joe might respond, "Tell me specifically what makes you think I can't take care of our children?" His ex's answer could clarify for Joe exactly what her concerns are.

Asking questions can also bring insight into what the other person intends to communicate later on. With that information one can better prepare for what is to come.

When asking questions, be especially conscious of the non-verbal messages you send. For instance, if your ex-wife is sitting, do the same. Towering over one's ex-spouse may make her feel intimidated. To be effective, queries must be presented respectfully — the quality and volume of one's voice, one's facial expression, and one's physical posture all have an effect on the person one is speaking to. An honest desire to know how someone feels and what he or she thinks, coupled with a non-threatening manner, goes a long way toward guaranteeing that there will be future opportunities to communicate openly and rationally.

If a father wishes to communicate as effectively as possible, he needs to examine the issue(s) at hand and to do so from a variety of perspectives. The more perspectives a father has, the better his chances of finding a fresh solution. Too often, men see a conflict exclusively from their point of view. Some, however, will consider their ex-wife's vantage point, and it is these individuals who have a better chance of resolving conflict than those who are close-minded. Understanding another person's take on a problem doesn't necessarily mean that you agree with it.

Creating a Shift in Perspective

Those who are committed to creating a co-parenting relationship must move past the defensive, angry father's point of view. Men who are successful in doing so learn to look at the larger picture realizing that their case will not be won or lost on any given day. They abandon their fears and, instead, learn to act and speak from a place of steady determination.

Once the initial shock of the divorce has passed, such men abandon the role of frustrated victim and become more grounded in who they really are as men/fathers — heartful, open-minded and confident. The first step in the transition, of course, is to get rid of one's anger. Once one has moved beyond anger, one can view a situation and the larger world from a broader perspective.

Here are three techniques that can produce a shift in one's perspective:

The first requires a change in one's physical alignment with the other person. For example: If two people are negotiating for *one* piece of rope, they are more apt to have a tug-of-war standing face-to-face than sitting side by side. Standing nose to nose they feel threatened; feeling afraid, they can easily overlook the fact that the two of them have something in common. They both want the rope and they both have only one perception.

One way to physically align oneself with an ex-spouse is to write a problem and a possible solution on a piece of paper and attach it to a clipboard. Let her read your suggestion while you hold the paper. Standing side-by-side, discuss what is written. Ask for her opinion, ideas and concerns. Write them down and discuss them. Do your brainstorming on the paper and the problem will no longer appear to be between the two of you.

To avoid misunderstandings, be sure to paraphrase. Paraphrasing is repeating back in your own words what you think you heard. For example if one's former wife says, "I want the children to be with me except that you can have them the day after Christmas and one week of their summer vacation." A father might paraphrase, "Let me make sure I understand. I can have the children on December 26th, and the week of August 1st through the 7th. And you want to look after them for the rest of the year? Am I correct?" Repeating what was just said can add a new perspective to a situation and in turn give both parties a better understanding of consequences. After a while, when your ex has had some experience of you paraphrasing, propose that the two of you use the technique to maintain cooperation.

Role-playing also can facilitate a shift in how a person views a situation. The process is simple. With two or three friends, or in an established support group, spend ten minutes a week role-playing. Begin by instructing someone to play your part in the upcoming situation. Now adopt the role of your past mate, and play out her part using her way of expressing herself, her gestures and her voice qualities. After that part has been played out, take your own position and act as you think you should. Finish the role playing by having people take on both your position and your ex-wife's. Step back, watch, and listen to the drama as an observer. When the role-playing is finished you will have a fuller understanding of the coming situation and can decide if the course of action you have in mind makes sense.

Having a thorough knowledge of what he wishes to communicate, and understanding that his tone of voice and body language matters, the speaker now prepares himself physically for the upcoming meeting. Certainly, what he communicates non-verbally is as important as what he says.

This two-part system can further enhance dialogue in a trying situation.

Part 1. *Cleanse the body and mind.* If a man attempts to communicate when he is feeling tense and his head is full of angry chatter, it is unlikely that he will be able to see and hear enough of what the other person has to say to communicate effectively. When a man is agitated he can miss the subtle, and often vital, messages the other person offers. At the same time his own body language, especially if it is signaling anger, may interfere with the other's ability to hear what is being said.

Use physical activity to release tension and quiet the mind. Weight lifting, running, splitting wood, or hammering nails all work well. While working out, verbalize your feelings. Express what is on your mind forcefully. Shout and yell.

Another way to quiet your mind and relax your body is to find a deserted area where you can shout out your feelings. Those who live in cities can go for a drive with their car windows rolled up. Express yourself thoroughly before meeting with your ex-wife, mediator or judge and you will arrive physically relaxed and mentally present.

Part 2. *Re-live past successes.* Remember a specific time in which you were able to call on your resources to handle a situation that was difficult or even dangerous.

In recalling that earlier moment, note how you were breathing, your posture, the quality of your movements, the sound of your voice, its rhythm and its loudness. **Study** this memory of yourself and all you heard and felt. Then visualize yourself moving to your image and putting it on like a skin-tight suit. Adopt the breathing pattern, postures, movements and voice qualities, so that you feel again as you did when you successfully handled that difficult situation. Now, imagine yourself in the upcoming meeting and visualize yourself speaking, feeling and acting as you did in the past when you mobilized your resources and succeeded. Relive those actions and sensations until you feel confident that you can again call up the resources necessary to succeed.

Clearing the mind and body and tapping into one's past successes produces a sense of confidence and that in turn helps a man be more assertive. When all the "facts" can be discussed in a non-threatening, confident and relaxed manner, conflict often lessens.

Speaking assertively means expressing oneself in a direct and sincere manner. A man can speak assertively without sounding disrespectful, aggressive, or blaming. There is a rule of thumb that differentiates an assertive statement from others.

If the sentence begins with "you" it probably will not be well received. For example: "You have been unreasonable from day one and I've had enough of you!" That sentence is blaming and threatening. A more effective technique is to use "I" statements. For example, "I would like to meet with you and exchange the names and phone numbers of the people we use for baby-sitting. And I want the baby-sitters to have both parents' phone numbers in case of an emergency."

When speaking be sure to use verbs such as: *feel, in touch with, care for, uncomfortable, afraid, love, need to,* and so on, in your sentences. Feeling verbs are easy to identify with. For example, "I am uncomfortable with Johnny's request for a car. His lack of self-discipline scares me. I'm afraid he'll hurt himself or someone else. I feel it's best to wait until he is seventeen before either of us lend him a car." When people speak in the context of how they feel there is usually less for the listener to feel defensive about. Another reason to use sensory verbs when speaking with women is that they may be accustomed to verbalizing their feelings and listening to others do the same. When a father mentions his emotions he gives this ex-wife an opportunity to identify.

Summary of Aids for Communication

A co-parenting couple will, in the years ahead of them, have numerous opportunities to use the communication skills in this chapter. To refresh your memory, and before each potentially difficult encounter, review the steps outlined below:

- Know in advance of the meeting with your child's mother what it is you want to achieve.

- Prepare yourself both by the cleansing rituals and by identifying and recapturing a strong positive experience from your past that has the resources you need to handle the upcoming situation.

- Align yourself with your ex- physically — sit or stand beside your past partner.

- Try to place the problem before the both of you, not between the two of you.

- Use framing in front of every communication (including the questions) to give your ex- enough context so that she can understand what is being requested or stated.

- Use questions plus paraphrasing to understand what she is proposing or saying before responding.

- Talk assertively and speak in terms of how you feel.

Parents' behavior is one of the principle determinants of what their children learn, how committed they will become as parents, and what kind of choices they will make as adults. Children are always studying their mothers and fathers — show them a dad they can be proud of and model for them the best of communication skills. Give your children every opportunity to succeed as parents in the families they create.

CHAPTER 5: MEDIATION

The Twofold Path of Argument:
The first path is learning the tools and moves;
The second path is concentration and relaxation.
One without the other does not work.

Michael A. Gilbert,
How to WIN an Argument

Family law courts prefer recording parenting agreements to ordering them. In most cases, judges order mediation and require parents to attempt to work out their own plan. Even in recommending counties, those where court appointed counselors interview parents and send them on to either mediation, custody counseling or probationary hearings, parents can ask for the opportunity to mediate. Many family law systems automatically grant parents three sessions with the hope that mothers and fathers will create their own parenting schedules. Most mediation is confidential, generally mediators do not make recommendations to the court or disclose what was said in sessions. When fears or hostility prevent parents from reaching agreements, the courts generally order them into custody counseling.

In custody counseling, couples are given a chance to create their own parenting schedule. If they are unable to cooperate, the counselor makes a recommendation to the judge. Typically judges follow counselor's recommendations and order parents to abide by them.

Fathers should initiate the mediation process. This demonstrates a willingness to reach a fair, expedient, and legal agreement, and at the same time allows Dad to take the lead in creating an agreement that is enforceable.

For example, if a recently divorced father has been the breadwinner of the family and now wants to co-parent, mediation is the place to start the process. His parenting agreement can include an outline of his plan to work progressively less and parent more. Men who say, "I'm not paying child support. I'm going to stay home with the kids like she does," won't be taken seriously if the children need the money he earns. The father must ease into working less as his ex-wife strives to work more. Often bread-winners need to allow at least two years for mothers to make the transition from homemaker to self-supporting parent. More and more mothers who want to hold fathers financially responsible indefinitely are being told by judges to get a job.

Jerry W., for example, two years after his divorce was struggling financially. He was caring for his children the majority of the time and paying child support to his ex-wife. His children's mother worked part-time as a waitress, four hours a day, two days a week, until the judge said, "I'll give you one week to find a job that pays enough for you to support yourself." Within a week, she was working full time. Eventually, Jerry and his ex settled into working part-time jobs and co-parenting their children for equal lengths of time. For the past ten years they have managed to work together to raise their children.

Working with Mediators

In most states, couples seeking a divorce will be sent into mediation. Many fathers are intimidated by court-ordered mediators and show up unprepared and feeling defensive. However, those who strive to benefit from the experience will listen closely to what the mediator has to say.

A wise father prepares himself in advance by speaking with other men who have been through the process and asking what they did to prepare themselves. Thus prepared he will feel confident in his plan and better able to follow up on suggestions.

Since mediators see numerous cases, if prompted, they may suggest improvements to parenting plans. At the same time, fathers should be on the lookout for agreements that are unenforceable. It is up to the parent to make sure that what they agree upon is practical, maintainable and legally binding.

A man we'll call Fred signed a co-parenting agreement with his ex-wife, Sheila, in court-ordered mediation. She was not happy with the arrangement, but kept her concerns to herself. Sheila and Fred were to parent equally — one week on and one week off. Fred thought all the details were covered. The judge approved their plan, and it was recorded. The next week, however, Sheila refused to abide by their agreement and denied Fred access to their children.

One year later, when the two stood before the judge, she complained, "It feels as if he's trying to control my life."

Having not seen his children for fourteen months, Fred asked for a contempt of court order against Sheila for refusing him access to his kids. He was denied because the mother's attorney pointed out that a clause in the co-parenting agreement stating that the children would continue to practice the Jewish faith was unconstitutional. Fred was Jewish and the mother was not. Therefore, the ex-wife was not bound by the agreement. Legally, it was not her responsibility to maintain the children's faith. With a red face, the judge conceded and suggested to the father that he return to mediation. All the judge could do was to remind both parents that their children were being harmed by their inability to cooperate.

A father needs to anticipate what his ex-wife might say or do and prepare to respond accordingly. After all, no one knows an ex-wife like a former husband. Those who are prepared stand the best chance of reaching an agreement in mediation and of getting a positive recommendation from the custody counselor.

Twelve Techniques to Enhance Mediation

- Situate yourself so you won't be distracted by activities going on outside the mediation room. If there is a window, place your back to it.

- Arrive for mediation ten minutes early. One father showed up on time and found his ex-spouse socializing with their assigned mediator as if the two were sorority sisters.

- Show up with an understanding of parenting options and have your preferences well-researched. Hard copy is best — for example, a visitation schedule marked on a calendar makes it easier for everyone to understand what the father's plans are.

- Bring a complete record — including canceled checks — for all child support payments.

- When speaking or defending your position, be clear, logical and assertive — but not aggressive.

- If your ex sounds blaming ("he's not capable of caring for the kids..."), ask, "What exactly do you need from me to co-parent?" You might also remind her that blaming undermines the opportunity to mediate. If necessary, ask the mediator to intercede.

- First impressions *are* important. When meeting with those who work in family law, show up well-dressed. Present yourself as friendly and professional.

- Stay focused on your child's needs.

- Don't talk about what the ex-wife did in the past. If you appear bitter or vindictive, you will be perceived as a parent who is unwilling to cooperate.

- If your ex slanders you, (use only as a means of establishing your boundaries and to motivate the mediator to take control of the session), in one sentence remind your past spouse of the most damaging thing she ever did to your children. Then immediately ask the mediator to "take control of the session." The point you want to make to your ex-wife is that you will cooperate, but you will not be a doormat.

- Be prepared with other options. What is the least you will accept? What might you bargain with or trade away?

- If you can get agreement on 70% of what you want, take it. You can work on the remaining 30% later.

More on Mediation and the Parenting Agreement

Clarke Dixon-Moses, a family mediator, shared the following observations:

> "Even in the most successful mediations, both parties often feel that they have given up more than they wanted... And the fathers that seem to do well in family mediations are those who show up with a daily parenting plan, a weekly plan and a outline for the year. When you see someone who is that prepared it's hard not to take them seriously.

> "Mediation spares parents a time-consuming court battle waged by attorneys charging hundreds of dollars an hour and kids are spared the hostile environment created by warring parents."

Courts that require mediation often hear complaints from parents of bias by court-appointed mediators. If a mediator appears biased toward the mother a father can respectfully ask for another mediator, preferably one who has lived the co-parenting experience. Occasionally the courts allow parents to change mediators. It is important, also, to remember that no matter how the mediation comes out, meditation itself is never the end of the process.

Mediation is a resource that can be used at any time. There are mediators who have private practices. Their rates are usually less than attorneys and, unlike an attorney, a mediator can empower both clients by encouraging them to seek what they want, understand all details, and look to the future.

When negotiating, prepare yourself emotionally, enter with confidence, use the communication skills outlined in Chapter 4, don't be influenced by emotional displays, and continue to insist on your right to parent your children. As a committed parent, you can carry yourself with pride because after all you are a dedicated father, someone your children can be proud to emulate.

Be sure the parenting agreement makes clear:

- Where the children will go to school

- What happens on holidays

- How the children will be exchanged (who drops them off, when and where)

- That the child cannot be moved out of the county, even temporarily, without the court's approval and the other parent's knowledge and consent

Stick to the Agreement

Don't waiver from the agreement unless absolutely necessary. Changing the parenting plan opens the door for confusion, misunderstandings, and resentment between mothers and fathers. For the protection of both parents, changes should be recorded with the courts immediately. Without a written record, agreements are forgotten, abandoned, manipulated, and become unenforceable.

For example, here is a situation that arises often: The parents have been bickering. Friday afternoon the father drives to his ex-wife's house to pick up his children for the weekend. His former spouse tells him that she is changing the visitation. She is going to take the kids to the park in the morning. He can pick his kids up tomorrow evening. The father is angry. He calls the police and reports his ex-spouse for denying him his children. The police ask, "What is the visitation schedule that appears on your court order?" The father remembers that the order, which has never been updated, allowed him to see his children four hours per night on Saturdays and Tuesdays only. He informs the police sergeant who then says, "There is nothing I can do without a court order and there is nothing you can do until court opens on Monday."

After a co-parenting schedule is recorded, continue to keep records of all financial transactions with your ex-spouse. Paying by check ensures you have a written record.

Changes should be researched and discussed with a counselor or knowledgeable friend before being presented to the ex-spouse for input. With good communication and mediation, parents can continue to minimize the impact of divorce on their children.

Consistency in the parenting schedule prevents children from feeling as if they are merely baggage being shuffled around at their parents' convenience.

If Mom and Dad have reached a mutually beneficial custody agreement without litigation, both deserve the others respect. As parents, they have demonstrated maturity, insight, and compassion by protecting their children from needless conflict.

CHAPTER 6: CREATING TWO
NEARLY EQUAL STANDARDS OF LIVING

If I had it to do again, when she said "I want a divorce," I would say, "Sorry to hear that. Where are you going to live?" I moved out of my home, when she wanted a divorce. Figure that. Now it's either put another home together or look bad in front of the judge.

Bob, divorced father of two

Couples who purchased homes while they were married must decide, once they are involved in divorce, what to do with the family home. If a father turns over his share of the house to the mother, she must now support a home that possibly took two incomes to sustain. If the mother gains sole custody of the children, which happens in the majority of cases, the added burden of caring for an expensive home can be overwhelming.

Renters don't have it any easier than homeowners. They will ask themselves many of the same questions that divorced homeowners wrestle with. They must decide if either parent can afford to remain in the dwelling. Unlike couples who sell houses and receive money from the sale, which they can then use to move, many renters have the added burden of acquiring the first and last month's rent before they can relocate. Still, divorced parents have to find housing that is sustainable if they want their children to feel secure.

Many mothers undergoing divorce insist on remaining in the family home. They mistakenly believe that the combination of child and spousal support will enable them to maintain their previous standard of living. Typically, however, the mother's standard of living falls soon after divorce. Child support very often falls short of the contribution that most husbands made when they lived with their wives and children.

Divorced fathers, too, suffer a drop in their standard of living. Child support is a major expense to add to the burden of supporting oneself. Reeling from the emotional impact of divorce and burdened with child/spousal support payments, most men become disheartened and frustrated — at least temporarily. And, as we know, some, "deadbeat dads," are so completely overwhelmed that they walk away from the children — the same is true for mothers who are ordered to pay child support.

Most fathers are very attached to their houses, yet some move out in the first days following separation because they think that a man is *supposed* to leave. Those who martyr themselves by moving out later become angry when they come to understand that they gave away years of labor and tens of thousands of dollars in equity.

The consequences of rash decisions — or unfair arrangements — show up in unhappy children. When parents are greedy or resentful, their children see it and are affected. If parents want to protect their children's peace of mind, then profits and liabilities must be shared equally. Fathers need to be realistic, courageous, and insightful when considering what to do with the family's residence.

Mickie and her ex-husband co-parented their daughter from the time she was six until she turned 18.

"Some divorced women," says Mickie, Director of Social Services in Santa Cruz, "hang onto their homes ferociously, even to the detriment of their children. These women seem to get all of their self-esteem from finding men who will try to take care of them. They don't seem to take pride in being able to care for themselves."

When parents focus on their children's need for stability, it may become easier to down-size the home. Selling the family's house can be a heartbreaking event, but as far as the children's future is concerned, selling may be the wisest choice of all.

Note: A year or two after the break-up, many mothers discover that it is unrealistic for them to try to maintain the family home by themselves. Still, there is seldom a need to put the home up for sale in the first months after separation. It's wise to allow time to adjust and adapt emotionally to a major life change. If it's inevitable that the home must be sold, then that need will become more and more obvious.

Three Common Scenarios Involving Homes and Divorce

Moving out: Many fathers undergoing divorce move out of their homes before they fully consider the consequences — including what it takes to create and maintain a residence suitable for their children. Bob, for example, is a co-parenting father with two children, a daughter, 7, and a son, 13. According to the court's calculation, his kids are with him 48% of each week. He moved out of a three-bedroom residence and now rents a one-bedroom cabin in the Santa Cruz Mountains. He works full-time in the construction industry, selling and installing scaffolding. His ex-wife, Bonnie, works part-time as a bartender. Because of the difference in their incomes, Bob pays $1000 a month in child support to his ex-wife.

> "Stocking this cabin with food and supplies is a time-consuming hassle — it costs lots of money and interferes with my time with the kids. I made four trips to the store last Saturday, just to buy things the kids and I needed. A needle and thread, house slippers, a thermometer, scissors and Tylenol, stuff I took for granted. If I had it to do again, when she said 'I want a divorce,' I would say, 'Sorry to hear that. Where are you going to live?'"

Currently Bob and his ex-wife are discussing what to do with the house. He wants to sell it and repay his parents, who loaned Bob and his wife the money for the down payment. Bonnie wants to keep the house, but she can't afford to make the mortgage payments.

Sharing the house: Some fathers believe they can work out an arrangement that makes it possible for them to share their home with the children's mother. Doug, a successful Realtor, and his self-employed wife had been married for six years when Dolores moved out of the home in which they lived together and took over a property they owned jointly. Doug and his children remained in the original residence. He has been trying to reach a financial agreement in order to finalize his divorce ever since.

His ex-wife cares for their children after school from 2:30 p.m. until 6:00 p.m., five days a week, at Doug's home. He looks after the kids from 6:00 p.m. until he drops them off at school the next morning.

> "I owned the house we lived in before we married," Doug says. "Now Dolores wants to move back and me to move out. I don't want her in the house because I'm not sure I can get her out. I was afraid selling the house would upset the children. But the inability to divide our property has hurt them. My daughter has started to yell at me, and my son told me yesterday, 'Mommy says you are going to make us move away and live on a boat.' Legally and morally, Dolores is not entitled to any of the property I owned before we married, but she won't accept that."

Remaining in the house: When Carol suggested John move out, John refused. He had invested every penny in the family home, and the mortgage payment was so large he could not afford to move elsewhere. In John's case, being financially trapped turned out to be a blessing.

While moving out was emotionally and financially difficult for Carol, she was the more capable of the two to make the move. She was committed to leaving, while John needed time to emotionally process the loss of their marriage. Carol believed separating was the best thing for their daughter and at the time John was unsure. Today, John knows Carol was right. They were not compatible, and neither was happy;

it was better to separate than to raise their daughter in an unhappy home.

Carol's mother, father, and her new boyfriend were all able to help out financially. Carol owned a landscaping business and John was paying $300 a month child support. She had the resources available to move, to care for herself, and to care for the couple's daughter.

If John had given Carol the house, he would have been on his own, and unable to purchase a home for his daughter and himself. Carol would have had such an advantage, both financially and emotionally, that John may well have lost his position as an involved parent. Certainly, he would have been unable to afford a home as large as she could provide.

John's daughter loves her home. She was born there and she is near neighbors who have always cared about her. As a result of his decision not to move, much of Alice's life is unchanged. She survived her parents' divorce with a minimum of trauma; her parents are emotionally stable, and her living situation remained secure.

If You Are Ordered Out of the House

Divorce is a frightening time for fathers, mothers, and their children. When parents feel insecure they often overreact — some have panic attacks, and others become emotionally, verbally, or physically abusive.

Daniel is the father of two pre-teenage children. He recently began his divorced father learning curve.

> "My wife said she was tired of earning all the money. Sally does earn twice as much as I do, but I'm the one who takes care of our kids and our house. Anyway, while she's yelling, she's pushing me, then she hits me — in front of the kids. That's it, I tell her I'm out of here. I left so that the kids wouldn't see us fighting like that. I pitched a tent at a friend's house.
>
> "About a week later, my wife and I drew up an agreement. I can use the house from 8:00 until 5:00,

while she's working. I can shower and use the phone. I am a tree-trimmer, and without the phone, I'm out of business. I agreed to give her $1,000 a month until things cool down. So far, nothing has cooled down.

"My wife and I argue every time we talk. A couple of days ago I thought, why do we keep fighting, so I bought two dozen roses. I thought that might patch things up. Ten minutes after I showed up, she was harping on me. This time she said, 'I'm taking the kids and we're leaving until you're gone.' As soon as they left, I threw the roses and the vase off the back deck.

"The next day when I came home to clean up, there is this note on the door. It said 'Daniel, there is a restraining order on you. You are to stay 100 yards from the house. I had the locks changed. If you come near the house, I'll call the police.'

"I couldn't believe it. We had a written contract that said I could use my house when she's gone. I admit I blew it when I threw the flowers, but I was the one who left so that the kids wouldn't see her hit me.

"The neighbor across the street said my wife is afraid of me, that she thinks I'm a bomb about to go off. Sally showed her neighbors the broken vase and told them to call her at work if they see me anywhere near the house."

Daniel's situation is not unusual. His wife hits him and he does not report her for spousal abuse. Later, he impulsively signs over the family home. Then, giving way to feelings of rage and frustration, he ends up with a restraining order and is labeled a "bomb about to go off."

Chip Rose reminds men that "Ninety percent of the time all she [the mother] has to do is yell 'alcohol abuse' or charge her ex with violence… or say to a judge 'I'm afraid' or 'The kids are afraid,' and the judge will say, 'Dad, time to move out.'"

Attorney David Ross has represented men and women in divorce cases for ten years.

"If there is the slightest sign that a man is unable to control his temper," Ross remarks, "the judge will slap a restraining order on him. Such requests are almost never refused. Men should not waste money trying to fight a restraining order. Judges tend to err on the side of being too careful. In the end, restraining orders make little difference. Some mothers sense a psychological victory, but clever fathers often get something from those orders.

"For instance, an ex-husband can say to his ex-wife, 'I don't have a problem with the restraining order. I'll stay away from you, our house, and our kids' school. Still, my kids and I do have a right to visit one another, and in order for us to do that, I now need you to deliver the children and pick them up for visits.' The same father might add, 'I would feel better if we exchanged our children in a safe place — someplace where a counselor could supervise us. And, I would like the pick up and delivery times recorded, as well as any problems. The records and observations might help us learn to work together. Also, I think we should split the cost for supervision.'"

This might feel threatening to his ex-wife, but supervised exchanges do limit the opportunities for conflict. Hopefully, she will realize that the smoother the exchanges and the fewer the fights, the healthier and happier her children will be.

Points to Remember
When Creating Another Home

You can sell your house or scale down your rental unit. It is often desirable to sell an expensive family home and divide the equity with your ex-spouse. In the long run, equalizing the standards of living for Mom and Dad, so that both have homes that are maintainable, benefits the children. Two sustainable homes allow for economic stability, a balance of power, and mutual respect for both parents. Of course, for each family's financial security and emotional soundness, both parents must be working adults. When only one parent works, there is no sense of equality and little stability.

If selling your house is the only way to create an ongoing co-parenting relationship, then sell. In most states, one parent can force the sale of the house even if the other parent does not want to sell. Fathers should research the laws in their state before attempting to sell the home. The needs of every family member must be taken into account, and the decision to sell must, in the long run, benefit the family as a whole.

Most divorced fathers are ordered to pay child support, and as a result, few fathers will have enough money to purchase a home for themselves and their children that is equal to the one they owned prior to separation. If the house the children and their mother live in is impractical, or costs so much that it stops the father from parenting, then the house should be sold.

"I have seen judges order that a home be sold if it interferes with parenting," reports David Ross.

When starting over, make sure the new home has plenty of space for the kids. Without adequate room, fathers have a difficult time convincing judges that they are serious about co-parenting. When children are small they take up little space, but the older they get, the more room they need, so plan ahead.

Judges may find it harder to make gender-biased decisions if the housing and parenting situations are equal. It is difficult to make fathers work and pay for the mother's home when both parents' standard of living is equal.

Demonstrating an understanding of what is necessary to provide for the children for the long term puts Dad on the same level as Mom.

CHAPTER 7:
MAKING SHARED PARENTING WORK

The bond that links your true family is not one of blood, but
of respect and joy in each other's life.

> Richard Bach, Illusions: The
> Adventures of a Reluctant Messiah

When parents separate and begin parenting independently
from each other, many discover they need additional support
from their community. Children must be cared for. They need
to be delivered and picked up from school, and supervised
while parents work to earn the money necessary to pay bills.
Parents who are already involved in their communities will
have an easier time making the transition to co-parenting than
those who have tended to isolate themselves. Setting up
appropriate child-care, maintaining friendships and keeping
children in the schools they are familiar with minimizes the
emotional trauma of moving out of nuclear families and into
co-parenting life-styles.

Childcare

There are numerous forms of childcare available for
children of every age. The means of supervision range from
hiring a nanny to forming a cooperative baby-sitting network
where you and other parents take turns looking after one
other's kids. When a father makes up his mind as to what he
feels will work best for his child, he can start looking for the
appropriate childcare. Unfortunately, there are more children
needing quality childcare than there are facilities with
openings, so many fathers find that they must be not only
diligent, but resourceful.

Dropping off your kid at day care is not always as easy as
it sounds. Most fathers have driven to the baby-sitter's and
have had their child burst into tears and cry out, "Daddy, don't

go. Please, Daddy don't go to work. Don't leave me. Daddy!"
Few situations are more disturbing. After an experience like
that, it's often Daddy that needs a baby-sitter.

More than once, after hearing my daughter cry, I picked
her up in my arms, skipped work and went home. After
missing numerous days of work, I asked my child-care
provider what to do. "Bring Stephany in with the other kids."
She suggested, "Tell her you'll see her after work, give her a
good hug, and leave. The secret is not to drag out the good-
bye. Dropping kids off is harder on parents then children. If
you want to, next time you drop Stephany off, sneak right
back and peek in the window and you will see that she has
stopped crying and started playing."

The next week I dropped my daughter off at the preschool, drove down the street, parked, walked back, and
peeked in the window. There was my kid happily playing with
another child.

For fathers who seldom see their children, dropping them
off for child-care is emotionally painful. Besides missing their
children's companionship, many feel as parents that they are
treading on thin ice. Ex-wives scrutinize the parenting of their
former spouses and if they feel the man's parenting is lacking.

Many, instead of coaching their former mates, will
withhold the children from them. Limited access to their
children and scrutiny can produce emotionally raw, hyper-
sensitive fathers who desperately want their children to be
happy. Making matters more difficult still, most divorced
fathers are ordered by the courts to pay child-support, and
therefore dads must balance work schedules with capable
parenting. If they feel the need to spend more time with their
children, and the kids balk at child-care, then the fathers are in
a quandary. Do they leave their crying children to go off to
work so they can pay child-support or do they take their
children home and enjoy quality time?

Some fathers are mistaken when they feel that the time their children spend at child-care is not productive. When children are being supervised at an age-appropriate facility they have the opportunity to play with their peers and this is at times more fun and educational for them than spending time with mom or dad. When the children are playing with their friends both parents are free to earn the money each needs to shelter their families.

Private Childcare: When children are too young to attend kindergarten and fathers need time to work, private childcare can be a solution. There are various types of institutions, ranging from commercial businesses located in shopping malls to individuals who supervise four or five children in the privacy of their own homes. State-licensed day care is preferable, although a license does not necessarily guarantee good childcare. Licensing does require that basic standards be met and, of course, it is always appropriate for parents to ask to see the child-care provider's license.

Most children seem to prefer the personal care offered by smaller businesses. The smaller outfits are usually more expensive, but many provide a more home-like setting. Some have a structured agenda that includes arts and craft projects. In the smaller, more private centers, there is usually a minimum weekly charge that must be paid whether or not a child attends.

The larger, more commercial facilities tend to be more play-oriented, and have a better-trained staff. The payment policies vary with day care facilities — some charge parents only for the hours used and others require full payment even if the child was not present for the entire time.

In many areas, there are long waiting lists for childcare. Working fathers often sign up for whatever help they can get and wait until their name comes up at the preferred day care center. Plan ahead to have the best chance of getting what you need.

After-School Recreation: Many elementary schools offer city-sponsored after-school care. The children remain on the school grounds and simply walk to a designated room where they sign an attendance sheet. Most after-school programs provide care from the time kindergarten classes end, usually around noon, until 6:00 p.m. Because after-school care is generally sponsored by the city, or the local Parks and Recreation Department, it is reasonably priced and well staffed.

Some city-sponsored programs have two levels of use. For instance, fathers can sign up for ten hours or less and pay a minimum amount. This works especially well for men who have flexible work hours and those who have children that may tire easily or simply prefer spending more quiet time at home. The fathers who must work later into the day and whose children enjoy spending extra time playing with friends after school benefit from the parks and recreation's full-time childcare program. Fathers should remember that school and play are as physically and emotionally tiring for children as work and parenting are for parents. Therefore if a parent's children say they are tired of childcare, when ever possible, the parent should take the kids home and let them rest.

Some parents who feel their children will benefit from additional instruction beyond the regular school day can sign up their children for continuing education classes. The continuing education program is more expensive than after-school recreation, but if the courses hold the child's interest, then the added classes are a bonus.

During the summer months, most Parks and Recreation Departments continue to offer childcare on the school grounds. Generally, Parks and Recreation will, because of the smaller summer enrollment, combine several after school programs and offer them at one location. The starting time is typically 6:00 a.m., and parents are expected to pick their children up by 6:00 p.m. It is wise to sign up at least two months in advance because summer programs are in great demand.

Sharing Childcare with Other Parents: After Stephany completed the fourth grade, I decided to work with two other parents in my neighborhood, Cathy and Annette, to provide childcare for our own kids. We were tired of paying for care, and our kids were tired of baby-sitters, so we decided to let them play at home under our supervision. The three of us began watching the kids on assigned days of the week.

Parenting every other week and rotating childcare with other parents means watching kids one or two working days every other week. Co-operative parenting worked well for me. My daughter was able to play with her friends and I was able to meet my work obligations. I would either take the girls with me or work at home. Adjusting my work schedule to allow for the supervision of three children for two days every other week was manageable.

When I had to work and could not personally provide child-care, I would hire a baby-sitter who met the pre-approved qualifications set by those in our group. Generally we hired a teenager who had been recommended by our circle of friends. When outside help was required we always sought the approval of our other parents in advance. Since we were from the same community we never had to hire a stranger.

The most difficult part of creating childcare by networking is keeping track of who is caring the kids and when. To avoid confusion each of the parents in our group recorded in advance of the coming week who was watching the kids on which day. That first summer I marked on my calendar the days I was to care for the kids. I kept the month's schedule posted next to my coffee maker so that in the morning, after my second cup, I could remind myself of what was planned for that day.

As the summer progressed, I was pleased to see that I was able to meet both my financial obligations and enjoy more time with my daughter. Saving $200. a month in childcare costs also brightened my days.

A reminder — Listen to your children. If they happen to tell you they don't like a particular baby-sitter or a childcare facility, ask them why. Your kids may be telling you that there is poor supervision, or even abuse occurring.

Watching Other People's Children: One of my daughter's best friends, Phoebe, then age 9, went out to breakfast with Stephany and me one Sunday morning. Her father, Drew, was to meet us at Auntie Mame's a locals restaurant. All went well until the girls began placing their orders. The waitress asked. "What will you have to drink?" Stephany ordered milk but Phoebe piped up, "I want coffee."

"Phoebe, do you drink coffee at home?" I asked, surprised.

"Yeah, I drink it black but with two spoons of sugar."

"Phoebe, do you *really* drink coffee at home?" I asked.

"Yeah, I have it black with two things of sugar."

My daughter sat quietly. The waitress looked at me with raised eyebrows.

"OK," I said, remembering Tim, a childhood friend whose parents served their kids coffee. Recalling that put me at ease. We went on to enjoy our meal and, as planned, Drew walked in just as we were finishing.

Phoebe, nearly jumping out of her chair, shouted, "Dad! Steve let me have coffee with breakfast."

Drew had forgotten to inform me of his daughter's recent discovery of caffeine.

Caring for other parent's children can be both a pleasure and a challenge. Co-parenting dads should always ask their counterparts if there is <u>anything</u> that they should be informed about the children being left in their care. And remember, no matter how closely fathers supervise children they will on occasion get the best of us.

Stay in the Neighborhood

Those of us who know our neighbors, and are friends with them, are fortunate. The people who live near us witness the growth and changes in our homes. Many care about us and our children and will support a decision to co-parent. Those who have known the family for years want the best for everyone. Ideally, they are our extended family. A father stands to gain much by remaining in his old neighborhood, close to friends, even if there is tension between himself and his children's mother.

Immediately after Dorese and John split up, the court's visitation schedule allowed him just two afternoon visits with his daughter per week. Reeling from the loss of contact with his child, lacking in confidence, and inexperienced as a single parent, John spent part of every day that his daughter was with him visiting his neighbors. They became a needed refuge and the visits lessened John's feelings of grief over the loss of his family and, at the same time, the socializing entertained his daughter.

"Looking back I see now that the people I was familiar with, were my support group. At their houses, my daughter played happily while I relaxed and honed my parenting skills. Our neighbors showed their support by their actions. An understanding smile, a cup of tea, or the invitation to stop by any time did much to strengthen my spirit."

Most divorced fathers can relate to the emotional pain that John lived with in those hellish days when his visitation rights were cut to a minimum. Without the help of kind people, like John's neighbors, the difficult transition into co-parenting would conquer more fathers.

In 1985, Patty, Tom, and their toddler, Alex, lived two houses up the street from us. My daughter Stephany and Alex were born only days apart, and from the beginning they played together. The two of them were almost inseparable for their first three years. Even after Alex's family moved twelve miles away, we visited almost every week.

84

Pat and Bob raised their two children, Robin and Christy, in our neighborhood. Following my family's break-up, my daughter and I were invited to visit anytime — announced or unannounced. Thanks to them, we always had someplace to go and something to do. The short visits with Bob, Pat, and their kids kept Stephany entertained and gave her a sense of stability.

I can say the same for Bob and Bernice, the retired couple who live next door. Their baked goods and warm greetings never failed to raise our morale.

Stephany and I have always found Rosie, the eccentric spinster who lives down the street, intriguing. Every other week my daughter and I would stop by for a visit. Rosie would entertain us with either tales from her past or her plans to embark on some future adventure.

I felt vulnerable when Nancy and I first separated, and, for a while, after a visit with our neighbors I would wonder if I was imposing on them. Was it rude to drop in every week? I often felt self-conscious and ill at ease, yet Stephany and I were always welcomed. The neighbors' acceptance of my co-parenting was empowering, and the support my daughter and I received made those difficult days bearable. The friendships I maintained with our neighbors benefited my daughter and I in two ways. First they made the transition to co-parenting less painful. Second, the regular calls we made to see them strengthened the bond between my daughter and myself.

Getting to Know
the Parents of Your Child's Friends

"It takes a village to raise a child" is an African saying made popular in the U.S.A. by Hillary Clinton. The phrase carries a message that can make a world of difference for divorced dads. Fathers who must move out of the old neighborhood can still help their children and themselves adjust to the move by initiating friendships with their new neighbors. Some fathers find it difficult to reach out when they are still hurting from divorce, and being the "new dad" on the block makes socializing an even greater challenge. Fortunately, kids are always generating stories and describing their antics can easily start a warm conversation. Many parents consider every day of their child's life fascinating and fuel for dialogue. If a father is willing to talk about children, he will never be in need of an icebreaker.

Dads striving to connect with other parents may find the following suggestions helpful:

- Take the initiative. Be the person who extends his hand and utters the first word. This can be as simple as sitting next to another father at a Tee-ball game and saying, "Hello, I'm Steve, Stephany's dad. You're Ryan's father aren't you? Do you know where the next practice is?"

- Open up to the mothers of your child's friends. Ask how they feel about the school, the teachers, or childcare.

- Speak **positively** about children, their interests, and upcoming events.

- When at sport activities, support all children, and congratulate other parents on *their* child's successes.

- Talk to other single fathers about the challenges of co-parenting. If sharing childcare will help you both, suggest that you and he work cooperatively when possible.

- On days that you drive your child to school, offer to take the neighbor's kid too.

- Be patient — it takes time and shared experiences to create trust and camaraderie. This is especially true when a parent is screening a new acquaintance and taking care to avoid contact with undesirables.

- Be optimistic — if you work to build relationships with other parents you will either build or join a desirable community.

For children, their father's involvement with other parents means more opportunities to play. For single parents, the greater the network, the easier it is to co-parent. The more people dads know, the easier it will be to find emotional and logistical support in the caring of their children.

Keep Your Kids in the School They Are Used To

School is a safe haven. There they have the opportunity to detach from stressed-out parents. In class and when socializing, peers and teachers demand the child's attention. There is little time to worry about parents or what might happen next week. And often, when children are worried at school, their classmates will try to help them.

Stephany and her girlfriends support other kids whose parents are divorced. On numerous occasions, when I picked Stephany up from school, she told me how one of her classmates had been feeling bad because her parents were divorcing. The child talked about her parents fighting every time they saw each other. Stephany and her friends gave the suffering student hugs and encouraged the child to talk about her situation. Kids whose parents divorced years ago shared their experiences and reminded the child that one day life would be fun again.

Keeping children in the same school they attended before the divorce will make the adjustment to co-parenting easier. There may be school counselors who have met the children and are available to parents for support and guidance. Teachers, too, can be helpful if fathers will open up and discuss the challenges of co-parenting in relation to their children and school. Divorced fathers can always use the parents of their children's friends as role models to learn new parenting skills.

Dropping my daughter off at school was a lonely experience when I began co-parenting. I felt intimidated by the happy parents and their cliques. I remember trying to start conversations with mothers and having them turn away, yet a few minutes later I would witness those same individuals conversing with their women friends. Disheartening and depressing as that was, I continued to show up and reach out.

87

As the years passed and I spent more time with my daughter, friendships did develop between myself and other parents. Now, most of the time, I feel very comfortable talking with the mothers of my daughter's friends, although occasionally I do feel like the odd man out.

Looking back, it seems that, the more school field trips I went on, the quicker I was accepted. Being packed on a bus with thirty kids and half a dozen parents can build camaraderie. Taking a class of fourth graders on an overnight trip will build unity between parents. Herding thirty ten-year-olds through a tour of the State Capitol Building without disrupting proceedings, for example, will provide both a sense of relief and accomplishment.

CHAPTER 8: FAMILY LAW COURT

Visitation is primarily the right of the children. They need to know that both parents will respect this right and are willing to support it.

Thomas Black, Family Law Judge

When Nancy and I first began our legal process, we each received a letter from Judge Black, who was to preside over our case. The three-page letter defined his role as a family law judge, outlined the mediation process, and explained why he felt it was important that both parents work towards a co-parenting agreement. What follows are some excerpts from that letter:

> "As the judge presiding over the Family Law Division of the Superior Court, I have too often seen how the anger, resentment, sadness and guilt that are part of many divorces affect the children. This effect is often severe and long lasting. It is my responsibility in these matters to protect the children and to keep uppermost in my mind their best interests when making decisions which affect their lives...

> "Both parents share not only the right of continuing contact with their children, but the responsibility for continuing their parenting functions.

> "In conclusion, be assured that a dissolution decree does not end your responsibility as a parent. Children need the ongoing affection, interest, and concern of both parents. The children must feel they have two parents who love them, even though their parents could not live happily with each other."

Judge Black is one of many professionals working in family law who are committed to children and parents. Most encourage mothers and fathers to maintain a cooperative relationship despite being divorced, and they strive to meet the needs of the couple's children. Daily, in family law courts, judges encourage maintaining ongoing relationships between divorced parents. As Judge Black goes on to say in his letter, "Your children need you both. They need to see you treat each other with courtesy and consideration. Although you may disagree about many things, your children must feel that at least you respect each other's right to still be a parent and to show love to them."

Parents who are unwilling or unable to work together are sent to mediation, child custody counseling, probation and so on through the ranks. As parents move through the divorce process, they are provided with additional opportunities to work on parenting arrangements that are in their children's best interest. Sometimes the process is successful and agreements are reached; other times parents fall into a downward spiral of conflict, court appearances and referrals by judges. Many divorced parents stumble for years before they find their way out of the system.

In addition to the challenge of getting divorcing couples to cooperate, those working in family law may be constrained or limited by: (a) the laws and the legal procedures that they must enforce; (b) their own personal experiences and beliefs regarding gender roles; (c) the large number of cases that must be processed.

The System Can Break Down

One afternoon, I checked the answering machine for the Divorced Fathers Network. The DFN is a non-profit support group in Santa Cruz, California, which is designed to help fathers through the process of divorce and towards co-parenting. On the tape was the panicked voice of Mike, a father who supports his daughter by working as a gardener. He had learned of our group from another father. The experience of Mike and his ex-wife, Gloria, shows how enforcing some "family laws" can actually interfere with the goal of providing for children's needs:

"I'm in a real scary position. I need to talk with somebody. I've had my daughter three or four days a week, at least half the time, since she was fifteen months old. She is eight years old now. Four-and-one-half years ago, my ex-wife, who has two children from a previous marriage, went on AFDC [Aid to Families of Dependent Children]. At that time I was ordered by the DA's office to pay $150.00 a month for child support to the state. I didn't have enough money to make regular payments because I only earn $15,000 a year. Now I'm in arrears $5,000, and the District Attorney is doing a five-year review. I've a court date April 25th. I can't sleep. I can't eat. I shake all the time. My ex-wife and I have worked together to raise our daughter for the past eight years. I'm a good dad. I'm doing my part. The Assistant DA threatened to send me to jail if I didn't pay the arrears. She said they were going to double my child support. I don't have any money. I had to file for bankruptcy two years ago."

Gloria, Mike's ex-wife, was also concerned. If her ex-husband went to jail, or the stress of his growing support debt overwhelmed him, she and their daughter would lose his physical support. "Even though we're no longer married, Mike still drives me and the kids to the store, the laundry, and to school events," Gloria said. "He is the most important person in my support system."

A few weeks later, as the AFDC laws require, Mike and Gloria had their five-year review. After their meeting with the Assistant District Attorney, Mike left the following message on the Divorced Fathers Network answering machine.

"I had my hearing today. The judge ordered me to pay $75.00 a month towards back child support. My monthly child support payment was raised from $150 to $210 a month, but I'm not going to jail. I'll take a second job to pay the $285.00 each month.

"Gloria lost the AFDC benefit for our daughter. When the judge and DA calculated how much time my daughter spends with me, they decided I have her 51% of the time and that Gloria has her 49%. Because Gloria has Tereasa less than 50% of the time, she's not eligible for welfare."

When the review ended, Gloria received less money from the state. Mike needed two jobs, one to support himself and his daughter, and the other to pay his ex-wife's AFDC bill. Because he would be working two jobs, his daughter, Tereasa, saw her father less. Their AFDC review lowered the entire family's standard of living.

Preconceptions Can Hinder Family Court Justice

Despite a real desire to be "fair and just," legal professionals sometimes fall short of their goal. In many cases they fail because their perception of life is based on their own personal experience. Seldom does the judge's or the DA's life parallel the lives of those who stand before them.

A judge who wishes to remain anonymous, because he is currently on the bench in a family law court, volunteered this information during a recess:

"When a father stands before me and says 'I want my kids half-time,' I think he's being unreasonable. Here is a man who a short time ago was working full-time, seeing his children evenings and weekends. He's divorced so he wants to parent half-time? I usually don't allow it. He's probably trying to avoid paying child-support.

"This court is gender neutral. Our primary concern is the child's welfare. Fathers are treated as equals here, but there is a difference that fathers have a hard time accepting. Here is how I explain it. When a child scrapes a knee, who does she run to for a bandage?

"The mother. At least that is the way it is at my house. For that reason, I seldom award fifty-fifty custody. It is

92

usually limited visitation — sometimes two or four hours a week. A lot of fathers have a hard time with that."

Many judges have preconceived ideas that interfere with men taking care of children. Dads who stand before prejudiced individuals have to be more patient and determined than those who face judges who understand that both men and women can be nurturing. Men who face biased judiciaries generally start their co-parenting with fewer hours of visitation. These fathers will have to accept that their progress towards full co-parenting will be slower than those who face a neutral justice.

Being forced to parent as the court dictates is a humiliating experience, especially if the judge knows little about the family before him. Men who endure that kind of humiliation, yet have the courage to keep on trying to co-parent, deserve respect.

Preparing for Court

To get the best possible ruling from a judge, fathers must be prepared for their day in court. Here are four areas that can have a major effect:

- Court room etiquette — tone of speech, body language, and appearance all can influence a court case.
- Divorce procedure — understanding each step of the family law process.
- Represent yourself in court — forgoing an attorney can limit conflict. Direct communication with a judge is the quickest way to inform the court of why and how you plan to co-parent.
- Hiring a good attorney — choose a lawyer who is skilled in conflict resolution.

Fathers can learn much by spending at least three mornings in the same courtroom where their own case will be heard. Each parent they see will demonstrate what is — or is not — acceptable. A man can see what works successfully and what doesn't. Within the first three hours a father is likely to see the negative consequences of expressing anger in court, the rewards of reaching an agreement, and the embarrassment that can result from being unprepared.

The first day the proceedings will seem mysterious. Later, patterns of cause and effect become clear. By the end of the third day, the cases are becoming repetitious, and the outcome of each is predictable. After three mornings you may feel comfortable in the courtroom, the judge has noted your presence, and considers you a concerned parent.

Following are three examples. The names are fictitious, yet the situations and dialogue are as accurate as memory will allow. (Tape recorders are not allowed in the courtroom.)

Outside the door leading into the courtroom, thirty people nervously mill about, crowds of parents, their friends, and attorneys. The mood is somber. Everyone speaks in whispers.

At 8:30, the court is called to order. The judge enters all rise and remain standing until the judge sits. Those in the court room are informed by the judge of the order of cases for the day. The parents who are new to the family law process and who do not yet have a parenting schedule will be called first.

They will be assigned an Emergency Screener who will briefly interview them, generally for fifteen minutes each. Her parenting recommendation will be court ordered and used by the parents until they enter mediation. In states where fifty/fifty parenting is not immediately court ordered, when mothers are opposed to co-parenting fathers are almost always awarded minimal visitation from emergency screeners.

The parents who have attorneys present will be heard after the screeners are assigned. And those lawyers with clients who have reached a parenting agreement will be first. Mothers and fathers who are in conflicted divorces are heard last.

Case One: The judge calls the first case. "Are Joseph and Marcie Smith present?"

Two attorneys and the parents stand before the judge. For the court's record, the attorneys introduce themselves and their clients. The mother and father are a well-dressed couple in their thirties. They sit at separate tables, and each has a folder before them. Their attorneys stand between the parents, and all four wait as the judge reviews their case folder. When he looks up, the hearing begins.

Wife's Attorney: "Your Honor, I am glad to report that Mrs. Smith and Mr. Smith worked out the final details of their custody agreement in the hall this morning. They have decided that Mr. Smith will care for their son, David, every other weekend. Mr. Smith will pick David up from school at 3:00 p.m. on Wednesday. Their son will stay with his father until 8:00 a.m., Sunday morning. The father agrees to return David to his mother at her home. Mrs. Smith is aware that the child support will change to reflect the additional time her son spends with his father. All of the remaining custody stipulations remain unchanged.

Mr. Smith has provided us with a current income and expense statement and his tax forms." (The attorney hands the financial reports to the court monitor who relays them to the judge.) "Mrs. Smith has looked at the statements. She believes the amounts shown are accurate." (Using a computer, the judge calculates the support payment.)

Judge: "I show the father will have the child 48% of the time. Support will be $525.00. Mrs. Smith, have you heard the conditions of custody and child support? Do you understand them? Are they acceptable to you?"

Mrs. Smith: "Yes."

Judge: "Mr. Smith, have you heard the conditions of custody and child support? Do you understand them? Are they acceptable to you?"

Mr. Smith: "Yes."

Judge: "I would like to commend you both for settling this matter. It shows me that you care about your son — that you are good parents. I can't stress enough how your ability to negotiate will benefit David. Keep up the good work."

Case Two: The judge calls the second case: "Are James Thomas and Sherri Thomas present?" he asks.

A stocky man in his middle twenties, dressed in a fleece collared denim jacket stands up. A blonde woman in a floral spring dress, follows her attorney to one of two tables inside the railing. Her ex-husband takes a chair at the other table. Her attorney speaks first:

Plaintiff's attorney: "Good morning, Your Honor. Patrick Goodman representing Sherri Thomas, who is present. We're asking that a restraining order be issued against James Thomas. On May 16th, James arrived at my client's home. He entered uninvited, and threatened her and a friend of hers."

James: "Your Honor, I can explain that."

Judge: "Mr. Thomas, you're interrupting."

James: "Your Honor, I have things at my house, where she's living now, that I need for work."

Judge: "Mrs. Thomas, does he have property in the house?"

Sherri: "Yes, he has three boxes in the storage room."

Judge: "Is it acceptable to you if he takes those?"

Sherri: "Yes, I don't care if he gets his things. But I don't want to be there when he comes over. He barged into the house and threatened us. I'm scared. I don't want to be home when he's there."

James: "I didn't threaten her or that guy. Believe me, I don't want her. Been there, done that one, Your Honor."

Judge: "Mr. Thomas, be quiet. That didn't help you."

James: "I want to say something. If I can your Honor?"

Judge: "Don't say anything else, or I'll have you removed. Based on your actions today, I am granting the request for a restraining order. Mr. Thomas, you are to stay 100 yards away from your ex-wife, her house, and place of business at all times for the next three years. Because of your lack of self-control I'm extending this order to include the children's school. Do you understand?"

James: "Your Honor! Can I say something now?"

The bailiff walks over and stands next to James Thomas.

Judge: "It appears that you are having a hard time controlling yourself. I suggest that you relax. The restraining order is for three years. Violate it, and you can serve a year in jail and be fined $2,500. Do you understand?

James: "I hear you!"

Judge: "Remove Mr. Thomas."

The bailiff takes James by the arm and leads him to the back corner of the courtroom, near to an exit. He positions James so that his toes are touching the baseboard and his nose is an inch from the wall.

Judge: "Mrs. Thomas, the order is in effect. You are free to go. Mr. Thomas will be allowed to leave the courtroom fifteen minutes after you leave. I encourage you not to speak with him in person and please do your part to honor this restraining order."

Sherri: "I will. Thank you."

By watching parents and judges interact, divorcing men can see how an individual's physical manner sets the tone for upcoming communication and interactions. Generally, when mothers speak in court, they are soft-spoken. They usually sit upright or lean back in their chairs. They tend to keep their hands in their laps. Their posture is non aggressive and typically cooperative. Conversely, men sometimes sit leaning forward, with their hands on the desk and their elbows locked. Or they lean way back in their chairs with their arms crossed on their chests. Many times anger can be heard in both the tone and volume of men's voices. More often than not, a father's body language suggests defensiveness, anger, or even aggression, none of which coaxes cooperation from family law judges.

As a counselor, Claudia Alonzo works principally with children. On occasion she testifies in court, generally either on the child's behalf or in conjunction with a parent to protect a child from further abuse:

> "The courts are loathe to restrict a parent's right to their children, and rightly so. However, I am upset at how some people can manipulate the system and look good while doing it. I have a situation where a three-year-old is providing the urine for her mother's drug tests. In this county, Child Protective Services is so overwhelmed, they won't research my claim. Because the child does not have broken bones or gonorrhea, the case is not a priority. Sometimes it's real hard to get action.

> "I think lots of dads make super primary parents. I wish the courts would recognize them more. Often though, if he is a dad who's not polished, rough or loud, the courts tend to look at him like he is some kind of a nut, and they quit listening. Let's say the father is outraged because he believes his child is being emotionally abused. When the father shows up with two inches of documents outlining three years of situations he considers damaging, the courts, at times, because he is loud and angry, don't take him seriously."

By sitting in on court sessions, fathers will hear suggestions that judges routinely offer parents. Their free advice can save fathers time, money and frustration. Some examples are below:

> "Mr. Jones, I have a full calendar and you are unprepared. We can't proceed today. I know this is a confusing process. I suggest that you get some legal help. The court monitor will give you a card for the Lawyers Referral Service. For thirty-

five dollars, you can speak with an attorney for half an hour. Even though this is not a criminal case, I suggest you consider getting some legal counsel. I'm going to reschedule you for sixty days from today."

Or: "Yes, Mrs. Peck, I did receive a letter from you, I have it here — unopened. Did you send a copy to Mr. Peck? I didn't think so. Mrs. Peck, I won't read anything unless it is sent to all of the parties involved."

When cases drag on for years, it is generally because one of the parent's emotions regularly get the best of him, and his actions thwart progress. Those men who control themselves and present their cases positively generally succeed in court.

Case Three: The next case is called.

Judge: "Are Tomas Martinez and Cathy Martinez here?" Two parents in their early twenties are representing themselves. The mother is in a pastel dress with a paisley pattern. The father is wearing blue jeans and a plaid shirt with a frayed collar:

Judge: "Mrs. Martinez, according to this report from the custody counselor, you have been, I'll quote here, 'entirely unwilling to cooperate and mediate.' Why is that?"

Cathy Martinez: "I met with the counselor and she was hostile. I won't subject myself to hostility!"

Judge: "I'm going to reschedule you, Mrs. Martinez. I want you to attend, and I expect you to work in good faith to resolve this matter."

Tomas Martinez: "Your Honor, this has been going on for over five years."

Judge: "Mr. Martinez, please don't interrupt."

Cathy Martinez: "Your Honor, will you extend the restraining order? I don't want him near me. I don't want him at my daughter's school, or phoning my work either. He called there and upset my supervisor. He can make me lose my job."

Judge: "Mr. Martinez, did you call her place of business?"

Tomas Martinez: "Yes, I did."

Judge: "Why?"

Tomas Martinez: "She wanted to change the time when I was to see my boys."

Judge: "Mr. Martinez, a restraining order has been in place for almost three years. You know you are to stay one hundred yards away from your daughter's school, your wife's home, and where she works. Now, you are not to phone her at work. Do you understand?"

Tomas Martinez: "Your Honor, I just want this to end! I'm missing work every time I come down here. How am I supposed to pay child support and provide a home for myself and my boys when I don't work? All I am asking for is to see my sons more. This is not fair. She is manipulating the court and abusing the law and playing us for fools!"

Judge: "Mr. Martinez, I want you to know no one is punishing you. I know this is difficult. It is not always fair. A restraining order was in effect though, and if you won't abide by it I can't help you."

Judge: "Mrs. Martinez, I'll schedule you for custody counseling six weeks from today."

Cathy Martinez: "Your Honor, I can't be there in six weeks. I am going out of town to see my mother. I planned that a month ago."

Judge: "Does eight weeks work, Mrs. Martinez?"

Cathy Martinez: "Yes, I'll be back by then."

Judge: "OK. I will see you both on May 23rd. Unless, of course, you work this out. In that case, you do not need to return. Try to do that much for your children."

Tomas Martinez's lack of control in the court room and his phone call to his wife's office forced the judge to shift his focus away from Cathy Martinez's unwillingness to mediate, an attitude that the judge does not support. After five years Tomas is short of patience, still his lack of self-control allows his ex-wife to both control the proceedings in the court room and make the mediation process drag on for years.

Keith, a father of three, worked his way through a very volatile divorce — both he and his wife instigated domestic violence, and both received restraining orders. Their conflict after their divorce decree continued for seven years. Despite his wife's resistance, Keith created a co-parenting arrangement that works:

> "Initially, I had four hours a week visitation and $2,000.00 a month in support payments. Currently I have my kids three and a half days a week and I pay $500 per month. Almost every time I've gone to court, I have had my way. That is not going to happen for everyone. Setting up shared custody is not easy, it's a grueling process. I believe I won because I'm a fair and reasonable person. I never asked for anything more than I deserved and I didn't give up until I got it."

Keith also kept accurate records, and, when his ex-wife was abusive, he filed harassment charges against her with the District Attorney's Office. Eventually a sheriff was dispatched and his ex-wife was ordered in person by deputies to stay away from her ex-husband.

A Few Things Judges Will Not Allow

- Insults
- Interruptions
- Angry outbursts.
- Letters mailed only to them
- Bickering between ex-spouses
- Lengthy explanations of past incidents.
- Discussion of issues not on the court calendar.

General Comparison
of Mothers and Fathers in Court

- Mothers usually come to court with a friend. Fathers tend to be alone.

- Mothers put thought into how they dress. Fathers tend to be casually dressed.

- Mothers are more soft spoken and mention how they feel. Fathers tend to be louder   and seldom talk about feelings.

- Mothers often request restraining orders. Fathers almost never ask for protection from their ex-wives.

- Mothers discuss their children's needs when they talk about child support. Fathers seldom ask for financial assistance for their children.

- Mothers rarely interrupt judges. Fathers sometimes do.

- Mothers do not assume responsibility for mistakes. Fathers at times sound like martyrs.

- Mothers often ask for the court's help. Fathers tend to tough it out.

Saving Time and Money

Twelve hours of courtroom observation can save a dad months of time and tens of thousands of dollars. Besides learning courtroom manner, and observing that there is a proper order for family law procedures, an observer can evaluate attorneys by their actions. As a result of watching them work, a father may decide which attorney to hire, or he may choose to represent himself. Still, though, to fully understand the legal consequences of decisions, to stay in sync with the order of procedure, and to understand legal documents, he sometimes needs legal counsel.

Before discussing attorneys, and moving on to special masters, the last in the line of the family law experts, a discussion of courtroom procedure is necessary.

CHAPTER 9: THE FAMILY LAW PROCESS AND HOW TO USE ATTORNEYS

The law is not an end in itself, nor does it provide ends. It is preeminently a means to serve what we think is right.

William J. Brennan, Jr.,
U.S. Supreme Court Justice

Judiciaries want parents to resolve disputes. The intention of the family law courts is to <u>assist</u> parents in ending their conflict. Judges are there to orchestrate the process by maintaining order and providing both parents with the same legal opportunities. Family law is far from perfect though and there are parents who will use the process itself to bludgeon former mates and in turn emotionally damage their own children. Parents who believe they will be able to enlist a judge's sympathies in their grudge match are mistaken. In their efforts to limit conflict, judiciaries will direct divorcing parents to one or all of the following resources.

- Family Law Facilitator

- Lawyers Referral Service

- Co-parenting counselor

- Special Master (not yet universally available)

A Family Law Facilitator is an attorney, available free of charge, to assist divorcing parents who have not hired legal counsel, with child support, spousal support, health insurance, and related matters of divorce and paternity. Family Law Facilitators are frequently located in the court house. Typically, half hour appointments are made on a first-come basis. Facilitators are paid with tax moneys to assist parents with legal forms and scheduling; *they are not permitted to give legal advice.* Seventy-five percent of people they serve are fathers.

103

The Lawyers Referral Service provides a consultation with an attorney for half an hour for a minimal fee, generally for less than fifty dollars.

Co-parenting counseling gives parents an opportunity to learn the skills necessary to co-operatively parent their child. Generally, when the court refers parents to a counselor the fees for services are based on the parents' incomes.

Special Masters (sometimes referred to as Guardian Ad Litems and quasi-judges) are officers of the courts. They have the authority to make decisions and to order actions regarding the best interests of the children, *except that they cannot change the designation of legal and physical custody.* The Special Masters Program was created to provide the parents in drawn-out divorces with a more efficient means to address co-parenting problems.

Here is how one member of the family law judge, who requested anonymity, handles the most common cause of dispute, the request for more time with the kids:

"If a father approaches me and says, 'Your Honor, I have a plan where I intend to taper off work. At the end of 18 months, I hope to be in a position to parent half the time. But I need my ex-wife to work more.' A man like that will be referred to custody counseling. Hopefully he and his ex-wife can agree on his plan. Unless there are unusual circumstances, it is not my position to order her to work more."

Parents who think they can use family law to "beat" the other person "once and for all" are mistaken. Divorce courts are not arenas where people win children. Unlike criminal cases where a person is sentenced and there is limited recourse to appeal, custody cases are always open for negotiation. There is never a final victory, other than an agreement between two parents to stop fighting and share in the raising of their children. The best a father can hope for — or "win" — is to get an equitable parenting agreement recorded. If the initial agreement is not perfect, a man can make a commitment to negotiate a better deal with his ex- in the future. Even in extreme situations — say, where a child is removed from a parent who is a drug addict — if an individual recovers from the addiction, he or she has the right to parent again. In many states when a child reaches the age of twelve his or her wishes are honored by the courts and that can change the parenting arrangement.

For most fathers in "conflicted divorces," the term for cases where parents fight chronically, the reason to go to court is to obtain a legally binding parenting agreement. For most men, early court orders are unacceptable co-parenting schedules. Still, all is not lost, because such a father can patiently work within the family law system to build a better arrangement for himself and his children.

How to Win More Time with Children

Here are ways for men to win more time with their children:

- By proving to a custody counselor that they are devoted parents. This is accomplished by providing the counselor with a written history of involvement that is validated by witnesses, such as the children's teachers, the minister or rabbi, and the family doctor and dentist. Further, devoted fathers can support their cases by speaking of the love they have for their children and then citing examples of contributions they have made to their kid's lives. Copies of all letters need to be placed in the divorce case folder generally kept at the courthouse. Case folders are a perfect place to preserve a written history of dad's struggle to remain a parent. The information within the court case folder is available to both parents. Copies of letters and minutes can be purchased from the court recorder. Keeping a personal copy of the case folder readily accessible limits misunderstandings about court ordered shared-parenting arrangements.

- By hiring a Child Psychologist to work with the children, and then asking that professional to make clear to the judge that the ex-wife's resistance to the father's co-parenting is harming their children. Say for example, that children want to see their father and are denied access by the mother. Many courts now consider it child abuse for a mother to prevent a child from seeing his/her father.

- By explaining to the court the specific needs of individual children. When a father knows exactly what his children need, and explains why he is most qualified to meet those requirements adults with the power to deny his children become morally liable. Few in family law have the desire to shortchange a child.

If a man wants to co-parent, and his ex-wife is opposed to his involvement, the father may have to remind the court of (a) the contributions he can make to his children, (b) the damage done to his kids by the former-wife's resistance, and (c) the children's emotional and physical need for two parents.

According to Mediator and Attorney Chip Rose: "The right to parent has nothing to do with whether a father has 20 percent or 50 percent custody. People's right to be involved with their children has to do with the small details. Dads who show up at every back-to-school night and don't miss a parent-teacher conference, those are the dads who legitimize themselves. They clearly rise like cream to the surface. In the professional field, family lawyers, therapists, and judges — those who are involved in contested issues — will immediately recognize an active and sincere father."

Men who are preparing for mediation or a court appearance should compile a concise written history of their parenting, and submit this documentation to counselors, attorneys, and judges, and ensure that a copy is placed in the case folder. Case files are available to parents who wish to read the court's minutes and want to check to see if legal documents have been filed properly. Personal letters are generally stored in the left pocket and legal documents are kept on the right side. Judges review cases before the parties appear in court.

Judges are influenced by parent's histories and most believe dedicated parents should remain with their kids.

Be sure to list every moment you spend with, supervising, or providing for your children. Some men make the mistake of recording only the "quality time" spent parenting such as coaching a team, attending school events, or reading at bed time. Time spent at home while children play at the neighbors, attend movies or sleep over at slumber parties also qualifies as parenting. Calculate the percentage of the week's total hours that you dedicate to your kids. For instance, were the children your responsibility 20%, 50%, or 80% of the week, and in turn the year? How might the courts view such a level of commitment to your family? If a father wants an idea of how a judge may perceive him before the two of them meet he can review his court case folder.

There are variations in how family law courts process divorcing parents. In almost every case, however, the procedure allows parents the opportunity to build their own agreement. Most judges understand that a pact the parents create for themselves will out last any the court might force on them. Therefore, judiciaries are generally hesitant to order parents to accept a ready-made contract. For that reason the divorce process can be time consuming, and there are often numerous points along the way for parents to mediate.

Here is a portion of the "Child Custody Dispute Resolution Process" for Santa Cruz County, California. Note that paternity must be established before this process begins.

1. **Stipulation Re: Custody & Visitation** - This is often a notice to the court that the parents have resolved their problem and want their solution recorded and made legally binding. Parties can stipulate to custody and visitation and exit the legal system at any point.

2. **Court Hearing # 1** - Parents are not allowed to testify. Instead they are ordered into emergency screening where a 15 to 30 minute interview is performed by a mental health worker employed by the county. A recommendation is made

immediately after the interview to the judge, and the parenting arrangement that she/he outlines becomes the parents' temporary visitation order.

3. **Mediation** - After both the mother and father attend a 3 hour Divorce Education Workshop designed to inform them of the potential harm their children face as a product of divorce, the parents are allowed to mediate. Under the supervision of a mental health worker, supplied by the county, parents are given the opportunity to resolve child-related issues, such as visitation and custody.

4. **Court Hearing # 2** - If no agreement is reached in mediation, the conflicted case is referred to either custody counseling or Probation. No testimony is allowed at the second hearing.

5. **Custody Counseling** - Is a process similar to mediation, except that the custody counselor makes a recommendation to the Court regarding, parenting issues visitation, and child custody. Judges generally honor this recommendation. Either parent can contest the ruling and return to mediation or custody counseling.

6. **Probation Investigation/Evaluation** - Is an in depth investigation of especially problematic cases involving serious issues and is performed by an officer of the court. A recommendation pertaining to issuers of custody, visitation and parenting is made to the Court. Parents can be ordered to undergo psychological evaluations.

7. **Recommendation Re: Custody & Visitation** - The appointed experts who provide Custody Counseling and Probation Investigation/Evaluation produce written recommendations to the courts and both parents. If the divorce is still conflicted parents attend hearing number three.

8. **Court Hearing # 3**- Recommendations made by the court's experts are read and generally accepted by the judge and become a court order. If either parent is not willing to accept the court's parenting recommendations objections can be heard.

9. Objections to Recommendations - Parents can address the judge and explain in a concise manner why they disagree with a specific ruling. Because the court's time is limited, judges seldom allow long explanations.

10. Settlement Conference - The process consists of a meeting between attorneys and the professionals who made parenting recommendations to the court. A **Judicial Settlement Conference** is an informal meeting where the judge and parents, (sometimes their lawyers and the court's experts) try to reach an understanding that allows the litigation to end and cooperation to begin.

11. Court Hearing # 4 - At this point a custody battle is waged in the court. Typically, testimony is heard relating to why one or the other parent should not have custody of his/her child. While many think this is the end of the divorce process it is not. Divorced parents can and often do drag each other back to court repeatedly.

12. Special Master - To limit litigation more and more courts are ordering the most challenging divorcing couples to use Special Masters. These experts, usually Doctors of Psychology, have the authority to order parents into conflict resolution programs, counseling, psychological examinations, psychotherapy or drug testing. Generally, they respond quickly to the needs of parents or children. The only limitation is that Special Masters cannot change a designation of legal or physical custody. They may, however, make a recommendation to the presiding family law judge about custody issues.

Most divorcing couples move through such a system in two years or less. On the other hand, some men and women spend five or more years presenting their cases to first one family law expert and then another. Parents who can't reach a truce with their past-spouses eventually become fed up with the system, and a few end up hiring Special Masters. (For more on this subject see Chapter 10) Those who spend years in the litigious loop of family law have forgotten a seldom mentioned truth.

Mom and dad are the key players in the family law process. They alone have the power to end their conflicted divorce and move on to co-parenting. When parents manage the process poorly, for example by relying solely on an attorney's advice, the family pays a high price emotionally and financially. In the many months that preceded the awareness that as parents they have the last word, many divorcing couples choose to hire attorneys. For a short time lawyers may be an asset. They can explain both legalese and the divorce process itself. Many parents feel reassured standing next to an attorney. The sense of security that some lawyers cultivate becomes a liability when parents forget that for all the years that lie ahead they, not their attorneys, must raise the children.

About Attorneys

Many attorneys share the views expressed by attorney Chip Rose:

> "A client walks into my office and dumps all of his frustrations, expectations and goals, many of which I have limited capacity to do anything about because I don't have access to the other person. I can only deal with the other person's lawyer.

> "Let's say the individual chooses one of the skilled attorneys with whom I have a good relationship. By skilled, I mean they are as skilled in common sense as they are in the legal process. In that case, the attorney and I would begin to collaborate on a professional level. We would put aside our partisanship as much as possible, and, while trying to represent our clients, look for the appropriate outcome, a solution that would allow each of the parents to move towards resolution without sacrificing principle issues. There is a small percentage of lawyers whom I consider highly skilled.

> "Parents who feel they must hire an attorney should listen closely to the what a prospective representative says. Grandiose phrases like; 'I'm sure we will win;'

'Your ex-wife sounds like a real jerk,' 'We'll make sure she's the one who visits the kids on the weekend, ' are red flags. Such statements signal attitudes that will prove expensive to their clients, that damages children and, from the prospective of most judges, is a liability to parents.

"There are lawyers who perceive their roles as helpers, and they earnestly work at it. They may not accomplish their goals because they have limited imaginations, or they can't see beyond the adversarial model they were trained in.

"If the other client chooses the 'bull dog' attorney that some friend recommended, a person who is into taking positions, then we are going nowhere. I am sad to say that is the norm. Lawyers like that are so adversarial, they create enormous conflict between the representatives. They take positions that are totally unrealistic. You have to take them to a judicial field and say, 'Judge, tell them they're wrong.' Attorneys of that type cause people an enormous amount of unhappiness.

"The clients who choose adversarial attorneys are without a doubt the caboose on the train. They didn't have a clue. They trusted the process because someone said 'You need a lawyer to protect you.' Attorneys don't protect people, and they don't take care of people — that is a myth."

Too often, in family law, lawyers try to force their client's will onto the other party. Divorce attorneys typically are seeking additional child-support, spousal support, or changes in visitation with children. It is not uncommon for these legal agents to work for women who demand full physical custody. In such cases a lawyer must be capable of convincing the judge that the father is not competent as a parent and cases like those tend to go on for years.

If one parent generates conflict, the other can ask his/her counsel to bring that fact to the court's attention. For example, a man's attorney might inform the judge that his client would like to return to custody counseling. The judge would most likely honor the request. Once in front of the counselor a man can demonstrate by a willingness to cooperate that he is the one who wishes to end the dissension and as we have seen many counselors will make recommendations to the courts that favor the cooperative parent.

When a father believes his ex-wife's attorney is interfering with the resolution of their case he can:

1. Ask the judge to refer the couple to custody counseling,

2. Use his own attorney for legal counsel only and represent himself in court

3. Suggest that the two attorneys use a third attorney as a stand in judge.

Some Strategies

- When a father tells a member of the judiciary that he wishes to negotiate directly with his ex-wife, it suggests that her attorney is unnecessary. When it appears to the person in charge that the parents are on the verge of working together there is a good chance he or she will send the couple into custody counseling or mediation. In a counselor's office the father may be able to convince his ex-wife that the person she hired is a hindrance to their progress and in turn a liability for their children. If his ex-wife disagrees, the father can always return to his own attorney and continue to fight in court.

- The father could use his representative for legal counsel only. With a knowledge of how to behave in court and an understanding of procedures, a father could ably present his case. Judges, knowing that parents are the ones who must ultimately raise their children, often prefer to speak directly to mom and dad. If the father presents his ideas effectively, and sincerely wants to end the fighting with his ex-, the judge may decide the wife's attorney is a hindrance. When that happens, the judge will direct his questions and suggestions to the parents and the lone lawyer is given few opportunities to express himself.

Contested divorces tend to be similar; expensive, slow, unimaginative legal contests that keep an attorney's client in ignorance. Mothers and fathers who avoid the stresses of traditional divorces do so by researching fresh solutions. Parents who are open-minded and flexible consider less common means of conflict resolution.

As an example, the three-attorney system works well for some. Each parent has his and her own attorney, who serves as a legal advisor. There is a third attorney, who acts as a judge, and speaks only with his or her counterparts. The lawyer acting as judge negotiates with the attorneys representing the mother and father. The parents make suggestions to their lawyers, who explain to them both the likelihood of success and the legality of the suggestion at hand. The parents' attorney's job is to screen out unreasonable requests.

When either party has a point their counsel brings that to the attorney acting as judge. The "judge" then relays the request to the other party's counsel, who in turn passes the request to his client. Suggestions go through the process; parent, counsel, acting judge, counsel, parent; back and forth until a resolution is reached.

At that point the attorney acting as judge writes the order for the parents; they present it to the judge in the court room; it is recorded and becomes legally binding. The advantage to the three-attorney system is that agreements and settlements can be achieved in less than an hour and it is common for cases to be settled in this manner in the halls outside courtrooms.

It is empowering to hire legal counsel when a father is unsure of the family law system but self-defeating if he ends up feeling at the mercy of his own attorney. To feel confident a man needs to ensure that he is on top of the process, well-informed and prepared. Those who do best remember that they are the key players in their own divorce process, their attorneys were hired to explain unfamiliar terms and a complex family law procedure, and finally to write up a legally binding, detailed agreement and mutually beneficial co-parenting contract.

Judge Kristopher Cottle, currently serving in the California Court of Appeals, has himself been divorced. A member of the judiciary for more than twenty years, he is soft spoken, direct, and the only judge I interviewed in this book who volunteered his home phone number in case of future questions:

"The most disturbing thing I hear from people who deal with attorneys is that their attorneys don't return phone calls. That irritates me. Lawyers are not so busy they can't return a client's call. When I hear that about an attorney I begin to have doubts about him or her. Family law lawyers need to do a certain amount of hand-holding. Their clients are upset. They're distrustful, they're resentful and, most of all, they're scared."

Many judges have themselves been divorced, or at least observed other family members struggle through the process. For that reason many have an understanding greater than parents give them credit for. Judiciaries feel deeply about the pain parents and children suffer as a result of an imperfect means for handling the break up of families.

Fathers need to be involved in their cases. Where possible they should work closely with their attorneys, who often handle a dozen or more cases at a time. If the father does not take some initiative his case might not get the attention it deserves. People regularly pay up to $300 per hour for a lawyer's time. Being proactive and involved in his own custody negotiation allows a man to save some of the financial reserves he may have acquired in his marriage and that benefits his entire family.

114

Lifestyle changes can influence proposed custody arrangements, and a father's legal counsel needs to be updated on all changes in work, housing, or health. Dads who observe in the courtroom will see parents reminding attorneys of relevant facts and details. When client and counsel work together, they have a better chance of reaching a resolution with the other party. Since ex-husbands know their ex-wives better than attorneys do, fathers know how much time his children's mother can spend alone with her kids before she becomes stressed. That type of information, for example, helps negotiate sustainable co-parenting schedules.

Lilly and Dale have been divorced for seven years. They are in their forties, co-parent Bryan, their son, and enjoy running marathons.

Dale imports clothing from South America and also buys and sells inventories from businesses that file for bankruptcy.

Lilly owns a successful clothing store specializing in beach apparel. Seventy-five percent of her income is earned in the summer and fall. During the tourist season, Lilly works sixty to eighty hours a week. She admits that without a prosperous summer and fall her business could not survive the slower winter months.

When the couple first separated, Dale explained to his attorney how important the tourist season was to his ex-wife's livelihood. His lawyer then suggested to Lilly's attorney that Dale be the primary childcare provider for Bryan during the busy summer season and that the parents reverse the childcare schedule before each winter. Knowing she and her son would have little opportunity to spend time together during the busy months Lilly agreed to the arrangement. The parents drew up a custody agreement and submitted it to the court to be recorded.

Five years later, Lilly, Dale, and their son are accustomed to the alternating schedule. Bryan is secure, happy, and healthy. Lilly and Dale are prosperous and contented parents.

Hiring an Attorney

When choosing an attorney hire one who you feel has confidence in you as a father. Listen closely to a lawyer's response. What he/she says will divulge how much that person supports your position. Statements like, "I would feel the same way" or "I don't think what you are asking for is unreasonable" can indicate shared values. At the same time, try to hire an individual who puts you at ease, someone with whom you sense a connection.

When a friend recommends an attorney, question him/her about the reference:

- Is she a "bulldog" or a negotiator?

- How long did it take him to resolve your case?

- Why do you think this person is the best choice for me?

- Did she listen well, keep you informed, and return calls promptly?

- Does he take the initiative or did you have to push to get the job done?

The stakes are too high to casually hire legal counsel. Even if a recommendation comes from a respected friend, a wise father is still cautious.

Attorneys have peak years, and sometimes those years net them reputations, usually as vicious fighters. The following year though the same lawyers can suffer a crisis or be burned out and in turn be completely unmotivated. Therefore, notice the physical and emotional condition of the person you are considering. Do you notice bloodshot eyes, nervousness, or fatigue? Does he/she look fit, rested, and relaxed?

Gather the recommendations and make a list, and then interview the individuals you are considering. Many lawyers do not charge for that first visit, and the mutual screening process that follows can help you both to decide if you want to work together.

A few lawyers charge $75 or more for the first meeting, and that offends many clients. Some say, "It's like paying a car salesman for the privilege of looking under the hood." Interviewing three attorneys who charge for every minute can easily cost $300 or more. How do you justify that kind of expense, and the stress and pain of rehashing your misery before strangers?

Look at it this way. Say you pay for three interviews and, as a result, get your questions answered by a variety of experts. Considering the seriousness of the issue, the $300 or so you spend might turn out to be a good investment. Further, if you end up with a sympathetic and competent lawyer, one with whom you feel comfortable, you are off to a good start and your money was well spent.

How Do You Prepare for the Interview?

- Assemble, well in advance, a list of questions you want to ask the attorney.

- Ask yourself: What is the best order in which to raise these questions?

- Clarify in your own mind what you want to accomplish and what you think your attorney can do?

- Remember to bring three or more letters from qualified people testifying both to your ability to parent and to your history as an involved father. *Documentation of this sort lends validity to your request to co-parent.*

- In addition, bring other relevant documentation, such as:

- Tax statements for the last three years.

- A current income and expense statement.

- An outline of the co-parenting arrangement you desire.

Remember, Appearance Matters

A well dressed individual with a professional appearance and manner is more likely to command the respect and attention of legal counsel — and later, of a judge — than someone who is overly casual and laid back. Show the attorney that you are reasonable, capable, and determined. Demonstrate to the lawyer by your manner and actions — and your advance planning in delivering relevant documentation — that you are a mature individual who is serious about placing his children's well-being first.

CHAPTER 10: SPECIAL MASTERS

When parents become disenchanted with the family law courts they can use a Special Master. Our process is more effective and a lot less expensive than going to court. The Special Master program won't empty the children's college fund.

Dr. Terry Johnston,
Special Master, Santa Clara, CA

Note: *Ask your judge if a special master program, or its equivalent, is available.*

Some parents spend years in the family law system before they become fed up with its lack of accessibility. When an issue arises it can take years to resolve it. In contested cases the normal process goes something like this:

A problem surfaces, mom contacts her attorney who contacts dad's attorney. Mom's attorney then files the paper work requesting a court date. The judge, parents, and attorneys agree on a date and it is placed on the court's calendar. Weeks pass but the problem remains. Finally the big day arrives.

Mom and dad, with their attorneys in tow, march into court. They await their turn to explain a problem to the judge. The parties want action. If the judge wants mom and dad to solve their own parenting problems the pair is ordered into counseling or mediation. This may, or may not, produce a solution to their problem.

If, on the other hand, the judge makes a ruling and orders one parent to change his/her ways, the problem still may not be solved. There is little that sitting judges can do to insure that the court's demands are upheld.

Family law judges are not supervisors. They are removed from the lives of the parents who stand before them and that makes it impossible for judges to insure that what was ordered is carried out.

In their book, *Don't Pee on my Leg and Tell Me It's Raining*, Judy Sheindlin and Josh Getlin suggests that the reader:

> "Consider the billions spent in resolving custody cases and their wrenching aftermath: Life savings are squandered on lawyers' fees, adding up to decades of debt. Court time taken up with these go arounds is prohibitively expensive. Money is spent on therapists for the parents, and therapists for the children. Special education is needed for those emotionally battered kids of divorce who cannot function in regular classrooms. Millions are spent on legal experts who testify to the venality of one parent or the other. We pay a huge price for all of this, in emotional and fiscal terms, and there is no end in sight."

How it Works

The Special Master Process was created to handle difficult divorce cases. Parents are given the opportunity to select and then to hire an individual to serve as their judge. That person is given the authority to make legally binding decisions — only on issues chosen by the parents. Having an authority who is readily available to oversee the parenting of children in contested divorces is for some a Godsend.

Special Master cases generally involve people who have histories of returning to court. Instead of using the court's resources they now rely on their quasi-judge. In almost all cases, the time, money, and effort needed to resolve conflict is less with Special Masters than it is to use the courts. Below are some reflections from Dr. Terry Johnston, a psychologist and 20-year veteran of Family Law:

> "I've been involved in the Special Master program from its inception. Initially there was a lot of controversy about whether or not a mental health person should function as a quasi-judge. Attorneys are not very open to non-attorneys being in a position of power. Their attitudes changed when they realized that

the new process gave them a place to send their difficult clients, the ones who wanted to return to court for trivial reasons and those who no longer have the means to pay for legal services."

The program was an immediate success. The most trying cases can now be handled as efficiently as possible. A faxed letter is all that is needed to contact most Special Masters. In an emergency his or her response can be as quick as a phone call. For example, let's say that a mother balks at fulfilling her parenting agreement and she refuses to allow her children to go with their father on a scheduled vacation.

If that father has a case with a Special Master he has ready access to an authority with the power to order the police to enforce the parenting agreement. In such cases the police are certain to take action. The children would be removed from the mother and turned over to the father. Parents realize quickly that the court order is to be honored. Dr. Johnston adds:

> "The Special Master Process works best coming into a structured situation. The couple needs to be at a place where there's some kind of custody agreement for two reasons. One is that it isn't really incumbent on a Special Master to decide who has custody. Mainly we help decide time sharing and co-parenting things. Secondly, by the time the parents have handled the custody issues they may have become disenchanted by the court system; maybe they're ready to turn to something else."

Finding A Special Master

There are various ways to find a Special Master. Most courts have a list of professionals that they approve of. Parents can also ask their attorneys for recommendations, or they may suggest to the courts an expert of their own choosing. What is essential is the willingness of both parents to give a chosen individual the power to make legally binding decisions for them.

Here are five points to consider when choosing a Special Master.

1. The minimum requirement would be maturity in the profession, at least 5 or 10 years of practice.

2. Knowledge of the Family Court System. The way to get an understanding of the Family Court System is to do evaluations, custody, counseling or mediation in the county where you are working.

3. It is very important that Special Masters be trained in domestic violence issues, and the kind of conflicts that come up in divorces.

4. Special Masters do not have to be psychologists, it's up to the parents to decide who they want. Whoever they choose needs to understand the developmental process of children and impact that divorce has on them.

5. Ideally the Special Master should fit the case. For instance, if both parents are highly educated, and a bit obsessive, the type who follow up on every detail, they will need a Special Master who is willing to work like that.

The cost of a Special Master is paid by the parents and is based on their individual incomes. Fees range from pro-bono to $150 per hour. Prior to the initial interview both parties provide one-half each of an advance deposit, sometimes as much as five thousand dollars. This covers future fees and expenses. When the case is closed what is not used is returned to the parents. If a Special Master prepares records or testifies for one party, both parties will share the responsibility of payment for that service.

The Special Master has the right to allocate payment for fees at a percentage different than the original agreement if he/she believes the need for service is attributed to the conduct of one party. When one parent is seen as the cause of most problems he/she will pay a larger portion of the bill. All expenses will be reimbursed and a minimum balance is maintained. Payment is due when services are rendered, and detailed expense statements are provided to both parties at the end of each month. Dr. Terry Johnston comments on the expense: "In 1993 and '94 we did some research and found that the average case that went to a Special Master had been to court more than six times in the year before. In the year after those cases hired a Special Master their average for court appearances fell to 1.6 times per year. We are saving the families and the tax payers a fortune."

Special Masters operate out of their own offices. The workspace is more conducive to conversation than that of a courtroom. There will be privacy, seating that is more comfortable than court benches, and the attention of a judge who is likely to know both parties well.

Because parents pay for the judiciary's time there is ample opportunity for mom and dad to explain the issue at hand and to receive detailed feedback. Attention to detail and adequate time for discussion increases the likelihood of successfully negotiating a solution to parenting issues.

Special Masters have the authority to make decisions regarding the best interests of children. Modifications to parenting agreements take effect immediately.

They are legally binding and will be recorded with the courts. **Special Masters cannot change a designation of legal or physical custody.** They may, however, make recommendations to the presiding judge about custody issues.

Here is a list of the Special Master's powers, although it may vary by state and/or jurisdiction:

- They have judicial immunity and cannot be sued or forced to testify; they may however choose to testify.

- They have the power to order parents to participate in dispute resolution processes, have the power to conduct informal hearings, need not comply with the rules of evidence or sworn testimony, and are not required to keep records.

- They have the authority to determine the protocol of all interviews, and who attends.

- They can order parents or children to participate in physical and psychological examinations, psychotherapy, drug testing and monitoring. They may make recommendations based upon conversations with parents, children, attorneys, witnesses or relevant writings.

Orders made by Special Masters continue to be in effect until set aside by a court with jurisdiction. All orders will be signed by a court judge at a later date. If the Special Master makes a recommendation to alter the physical or legal custody, the decision will not be effective until entered by the court as an order. An objecting party will have the burden of proof as to why the recommendation should not be adopted.

Either party, their attorney, or witnesses can contact a Special Master in writing provided that copies are delivered to the other parties involved simultaneously. Parties shall supply all records, documentation and information requested by a Special Master.

Special Masters mediate and negotiate only issues that are brought to them. When the mother and father cannot come to an agreement on their own then a decision is made for them. Excluding issues that endanger children, only matters that have been stipulated and agreed upon by both parents can be ruled on by their Special Master. Dr. Terry Johnston adds:

> "I don't want parents to give me the right to make decisions I don't need to make. Because, I don't want them to give away any more than they need to, except in the rare cases where the parents stipulate, Special Masters don't make custody decisions or decide money issues. The most important thing is that Special Masters do not go out to discover problems. If we don't like a parenting agreement it is not our job to set out to change it. The Special Master is a quasi-judicial role; we look only at what comes to us."

If divorced parents sincerely want to end their arguing, and they are competent parents who have gone to great lengths to select a fair Special Master then they should feel secure in the authority they have hired. Many parents though do feel afraid to hire a Special Master and sometimes for good reasons. According to retired family judge Judy Sheindlin, who served 24 years on the bench in New York City, "Courts are supposed to approach cases of child custody, support payments or visitation rights in what we call a gender-neutral posture. It sounds fair, and it is fair. But it is a myth. Judges are not enforcing these gender laws fairly, and few seem to care."

Selecting or Removing Special Masters

Special Masters can have gender bias. Therefore, it is critical that fathers interview in-depth potential Special Masters. It is acceptable to ask for references and then to phone them. When time is invested there is much you can learn about the professional that is being considered.

Many parents believe that once you sign a contract with a Special Master you are stuck with them, this is not the case. If a father encounters gender bias he can have the quasi-judge disqualified on any of the grounds applicable to the removal of a judge, referee or arbitrator.

Common causes for disqualification are allegations of bias, unethical conduct, unfair billing, malpractice, or other complaints regarding the performance of their duties. The removal process is often time-consuming, expensive, and stressful. A typical procedure for removing a Special Master is:

1. Discuss the grievance in person with the Special Master.

2. Submit a written letter detailing the complaint to all parties and their attorneys. The Special Master will then submit a written response to all involved.

3. The Special Master will then meet with the complaining party and his/her attorney to discuss the matter. A letter

by the party will follow that states whether or not the grievance is resolved.

4. If the problem is not resolved the Special Master will meet with both parties and their attorneys and attempt to resolve the matter.

5. If the complaint is not resolved, the complaining party may proceed by "noticed motion to the Court for the removal of the Special Master."

6. The Court shall reserve jurisdiction to determine if either or both parties and or the Special Master is ultimately responsible for any or all of the Special Master's time and costs spent in responding to the grievance.

In many states, upon notice of impending resignation, the Special Master is required to recommend to the parents at least three qualified replacements. A new Special Master shall be agreed upon by both parents or their Judge will assign them one. If the judge who has jurisdiction feels that the parents have acquired the ability to care for their children and remain out of court the parents may forgo the Special Master Process.

Acting as buffers for the divorcees in contested cases, Special Masters in many cases create the time and space necessary for parents to learn the skills needed to act civilly with one another. Sometimes it takes an ever-present authority to maintain peace long enough for tensions to evaporate and trust to develop.

A divorced father who is conscientiously working with a fair and knowledgeable Special Master should be, by all stretches of the imagination, assured his position as a parent. Now he and his children's mother have an opportunity to work with an ally to maintain their shared parenting relationship. As time passes, the parents, their children and the Special Master can become familiar with each other.

When divorced parents work to improve their skills and their referee is fair, then mutual respect develops. Parents feel secure about the wellbeing of their children knowing that they have the direct supervision of a legal authority. The conditions of the custody agreement will be honored by both parents. Misunderstandings and disagreements will be quickly researched and when needed prompt action taken. The results of a job well done by a Special Master is the de-escalation of tension between parents and more stability within the family.

In Conclusion

It is hard for cynics to support the idea that men are not committed parents when fathers maintain co-parenting arrangements and demonstrate that they love their offspring and are willing to go to any lengths to provide for them. Those who nurture their progeny not only help their children, they also fulfill a social need. The committed divorced father who maintains co-parenting demonstrates a new reality — he supports a new belief, and he offers another option to all parents. When mom and dad maintain co-parenting, the family doesn't end with divorce.

PART II:
THE MAINTENANCE OF CO-PARENTING

I expect that fathers can nurture their children just like mothers can nurture their children. We constantly put all the weight [of nurturing] onto the female, I want to take some of the weight off her and put it on the father, and I want to take some of the financial weight off the father and put it on the mother.

--Eloise Anderson,
Director of California's
Department of Social Services

CHAPTER 11: ADDRESSING SOME IMPORTANT ISSUES

When parents settle on a co-parenting agreement and it is recorded in court both mother and father feel a sense of relief. It's true they have endured a lot. Surviving the divorce and the custody dispute are major accomplishments, but there is still a greater challenge. The job of fostering cooperation through the years it takes to raise the children to adulthood still lies ahead.

Four Distractions to Co-Parenting

Four distractions upset the equilibrium of many co-parenting households:

- Isolation lulls fathers into a false sense of security.
- The obligation of work can distract the best of fathers.
- Dating others stresses the relationship between ex-spouses.
- Family emergencies intensify the parents' need to communicate.

The four forces outlined above often pull parents' attention away from their families and as a result relationships between parents can break down. For example, no competent mother would allow her ex-husband to place work before his children's needs.

Once a father's right to co-parent is recorded in court his attention must shift to the maintenance of his arrangement. Even if he is unhappy with what the court stipulates he must still maintain it. Only when he proves he can do what the judge wants him to do will he have a chance to improve his lot. Even those who are delighted with their schedules have to shift their focus; they too have to think in terms of the maintenance of their lifestyles if they want the arrangement to last until their child is an adult.

To sustain co-parenting there must be a conscientious shift in the way a father thinks. In the beginning when he is struggling to establish himself he has to think as a chess player might calculating each move in order to strengthen his own position and limit the ex-wife's moves. Once he has his parenting agreement in hand he can focus on sustaining his family. By using common sense, practicality and self-improvement a father can protect his position in the new family structure.

Men who work too much or who expose their children to their excessive dating (too many partners, inappropriate actions in front of children, dating too often, and so forth) are sure to trigger negative responses from their ex-wives. Fathers will know what is likely to trigger their ex-wives. If their ex is concerned about the welfare of her children when they are at their father's house, it is almost certain that both parents will end up back in court. Even men who had cooperative ex-wives from the beginning can fail at co-parenting if they don't make a conscientious effort to parent well. These failures are doubly painful for men: not only do their families suffer again, but their failures negatively influence judges and that negatively affects other co-parenting cases.

Watching fathers fight to win shared custody agreements, then seeing some of those fathers fail at maintaining what they struggled for, leads some judges to believe it is impossible for divorced couples to maintain co-parenting.

The judge who wishes to remain anonymous had this to say: "I haven't seen one co-parenting couple succeed."

He is being unreasonable when he assumes that none of the divorced mothers and fathers can learn to cooperatively raise their children. Unfortunately, judges who believe that co-parenting will fail often make decisions that support their beliefs. Typically, they try to reduce fathers to visitors.

Changing the Beliefs of Judges

So, how can we change their beliefs? The solution is to expose judges to the many co-parents who succeed. Every divorced father who is working with his ex-wife could write to the judge who handled their case; once a year should be enough. Remind him that you and your wife are still parenting, that life is good and your kids are happy. The letter may challenge his belief and will keep your name fresh in his mind: that could serve you if you stand before him again.

According to *CNN News* there are 1.6 million single-parent families headed by fathers and "The number is growing at a biblical rate." Single-parent families headed by fathers is the fastest growing family group in America. There are over a million divorces each year and if each successfully co-parenting father were to write, well, that might change some opinions. It would be hard to ignore a mountain of letters that read like this:

Dear Judge Black,

With each passing year my ex-wife and I communicate better. This year, five years after we bickered in your courtroom, we went on our daughter's school whale-watching trip together. Jewels loved having both of her parents share the outing. In many ways my relationship with her mother is better today than ever before. Jewels is all the proof Diane and I need that co-parenting works. I want to stress the importance of keeping both parents involved in their child's life.

Please do all you can to help other divorcing couples remain involved with their children.

Sincerely,
Daniel A. Divine

Fortunately, not every judge is like the "anonymous" judge. The Honorable Charles Kobayashi was the keynote speaker at the *Fathers Symposium*, February 8, 1997. He was introduced as the "The Judge of the Year for 1995."

Judge Kobayashi presides over a family law court in Sacramento, California. In his opening remarks he encouraged fathers "to remain involved because your children need you."

Later we were told that:

- All of their mediators are trained in gender bias avoidance.
- 85% of cases will be resolved in 3 to 5 mediation sessions.
- Only 5% of Sacramento's divorce cases ever go to trial.
- In 70% of the cases neither parent hires an attorney.
- The typical case costs 75 to 100 dollars to resolve.

Of course not all judges are as efficient as The Honorable Judge Kobayashi and not all family law systems are as progressive as those in Sacramento, California.

There are three things a divorced father can do to maintain his arrangement:

- Continue to work with other fathers.
- Make sure the child's wellbeing remains a priority.
- Continue to improve the communication with his ex-wife.

A father must practice the skills necessary to maintain his co-parenting. Nurturing the dialogue with his ex-wife, watching for dysfunction within their families and continuing to work with other fathers will enable him to deal with the four areas that cause most problems.

Once again, fathers must always remember that isolation, overworking, improper boundaries around dating and family emergencies are all wedges that can splinter co-parenting relationships.

CHAPTER 12:
AVOIDING THE ISOLATION TRAP

A friend is one who warns you.
Near East proverb

In *Surviving the Breakup*, authors Joan Kelly & Judith Wellerstein state that approximately 50% of divorced mothers "see no value in the father's continued contact with his children." Some men who would like to parent throughout their children's lives will not be allowed to because some mothers will interfere. The ex-husbands of women who are not committed to co-parenting are in a perilous position. If they want to co-parent they need to do everything within their power to maintain a working relationship with their ex-wives. It is extremely difficult to maintain a relationship with someone who is uncooperative. The men who succeed reach out to others for support and training. Those who isolate generally fail.

There are two reasons that fathers who isolate themselves are likely to lose their rights to co-parent:

First, during the years it takes for a child to grow into an adult, co-parents are sure to disagree intensely at times. Any number of situations can trouble them and in turn stress their relationship. As a result the parents may at times feel burned out, resentful, or frightened of one another. In any of those states an ex-wife can be uncooperative. Ex-husbands who are striving to maintain trying relationships under difficult conditions will at times need encouragement. They will also need fresh input in order develop new and better communication skills. Listening to the varied and ever-increasing experiences of other divorced fathers allows men the opportunity to grow in order to deal with their challenges.

Friends also can serve as buffers. For example, when something frightening happens friends can be the vehicles that help to release emotion. Expressing frustration, fears and anger to friends often means that ex-husbands do not have to dump their feelings onto their ex-wives. Seldom will ex-wives continue cooperating with those who leave them feeling bad.

Occasionally both parents will be on edge. The simplest situation can lead to an argument. This is especially true when the task at hand is inherently stressful. If parents become lax the most ordinary events can cause emotions to flare. Ask any kid with divorced parents and you'll get an example:

An Example of Detrimental Isolation

Roger has been co-parenting Ricky, his 12-year-old, with his ex-wife Bonnie for the last ten years on a fifty-fifty basis. Roger married Meredith five years ago. At that point Meredith began shielding Roger from his ex-wife and he began isolating himself.

Here is how Bonnie sees the latest situation:

"Since I have never claimed my son as a tax deduction I decided to do it this year. When I told Meredith they went nuts. She told me not to do that because it would mess up their taxes. That the IRS would audit them. She told me I was crazy for thinking such a thing. Then Meredith said she and Roger had enough of this co-parenting. That if I claimed Ricky as a dependent they were going to hire an attorney.

I don't get it. I've bent over backwards for them. I've done everything to get along. I haven't filed for child support and I could have. I know I could get it. I've had to talk with Meredith. My kid's father won't even talk with me. I've had to put up with that for five years. Do you know how that makes me feel? It hurts! Now they're threatening to hire an attorney. They both earn twice as much money as I do and I haven't asked for a penny, not one penny, ever. I let them claim Ricky every year. Do they say thank you, NO! They live in a big house and Ricky and I share a one-room apartment. Is that fair? No. And they're telling me I'm crazy because I want to claim my son for one year. I want a $2,250 deduction once and I'm crazy. We'll see who's crazy."

The lack of consideration by this father felt hurtful to the mother. By isolating he failed to improve his relationship with his ex-wife. If he had spoken with other fathers about his situation, someone would have told him that he had a cooperative ex-wife and that he should do everything within his power to get along. Few ex-wives share custody and ignore the child support and tax deductions they are entitled to. Also, refusing to speak with an ex-wife is insulting. (Imagine it the other way around.) Insisting that she converse with the stepmother was asking for trouble.

Discussing plans with others before taking action helps fathers avoid decisions that hurt and frighten their ex-wives. Parents generally seek sole physical and legal custody of a child when they feel insecure or they sense a chance to seize control.

If one adult is isolating but the other is reaching out to friends, the parent who is discussing pertinent issues can often mend an unhappy situation. If parents are not looking for solutions outside of themselves then their relationship is almost sure to fail. When both parents are searching for tools that will enable them to handle the ongoing challenge of working together, they are almost sure to succeed in maintaining their two homes.

Isolation Led to Mistakes... a Father's Reflections After the Fact

Dawain's weathered face, sinewy frame, and shoulder length hair accent his quick and confident smile. He is a landscape foreman who, today, has a "tolerable" relationship with Sarah, his ex-wife. From 1987 to 1993, they co-parented Tanya, their daughter, and the arrangement worked well.

Sarah did business overseas, and while she was away Tanya stayed with her dad. Dawain cared for their daughter for most of Tanya's first six years.

At the beginning of the seventh year Sarah's company offered her a new sales territory. She was to cover the West Coast: Oregon, Washington and California. Since Sarah would be in town more, she and Dawain decided to share Tonya's time equally.

Soon after they changed their parenting schedule, Dawain's father died. The death was unexpected and proved to be a major blow. Dawain had lost his best friend. While he grieved over the loss of his father major changes occurred at work. The owners chose to restructure the management. When the shuffling ended Dawain was told to work under someone he did not respect. Feeling lonely and dissatisfied he became depressed. Within a year the depression was so severe it affected his health.

"I decided that I needed a six month leave of absence from work and I asked Sarah if she would watch Tanya for six months. My plan was to rest until I felt better and then to resume parenting as before, 50/50.

"I told Sarah and Tanya what I had in mind and both of them were supportive. The company gave me a leave. I explained to the court what I wanted to do and the judge OK'd it. He even recorded the agreement Sarah and I signed.

"I thought all was in order so I looked forward to the rest. I had worked a long time and never took six months off.

"One month after my sabbatical began Sarah filed for full physical and legal custody of Tanya. She wanted absolute control. I didn't know what to do. I needed more rest, but the heart of my functioning was my child.

"When Sarah went after Tanya I told her to forget it, that I wouldn't allow it to happen. So she turned up the heat. She took Tanya to see a counselor and this counselor recommended that my daughter stay full time with her mother. When I objected, the counselor didn't want to hear my side of the story.

"Then, the same judge who granted me a six month leave of absence, on this counselor's recommendation, granted Sarah full custody of my daughter.

"Everything went so smoothly for Sarah. Her attorney said all the right things. My attorney seemed surprised all the time and then he would be slow to respond. A couple of months into it, after Sarah had won custody, Tanya, my daughter, asked me if I was going to withdraw my love. I told her I would never do that, and I asked her why would she ask me such a thing? She said, 'Mom said she would if I told the counselor I wanted to stay with you.' God, I was so pissed! There was no way I could leave my daughter with her mother now.

"We fought for three more years, until we both were broke. Still, I wasn't going to quit. When the final ruling came down the judge reversed his previous ruling and awarded me full custody of Tanya. It was because I was physically more available than her mother. During our custody battle Sarah's company had closed the West Coast area and reassigned her to the overseas area. Sarah chose to stay with her career, which meant traveling. I'm physically present so the courts awarded me custody. Throughout this whole ordeal I never knew how it was going to end.

"Looking back, I made some major mistakes. Asking Sarah to watch Tanya when I was depressed was stupid. Letting work drag me down wasn't too bright either, but not having anyone to bounce my ideas off of, that was what really started it all. When I realized I had distanced myself from counsel it was too late, the ball was rolling. After that all of Sarah's and my choices were poor ones and we all paid dearly for each of those mistakes. Tanya's in counseling trying to make sense of it all. Her mother and I don't trust each other and we're both in debt."

Maintenance Requires Discipline

It often appears to be unnecessary to discuss your decisions with friends, especially when life is easy and the right choices seem obvious. Still, the rewards of seeking support far outweigh the inconvenience. Sharing your plans with a friend might at the time seem pointless, but anything you do to avoid a custody battle is worth doing. Here are two more reasons why it pays to maintain contact with other dads:

Speaking regularly with divorced fathers keeps your memory fresh. Once those old pains are remembered the reason for checking with friends becomes as clear as a restraining order — never again do we want to relive the tumultuous time that follows most marital breakups. Without occasional reminders too many forgot to remain vigilant, and too often the past is relived.

Discussing the challenges he has faced with others allows a father to know in advance what his children may encounter as they grow. And on the other hand, hearing how others have dealt with problems gives a father the opportunity to avoid similar mistakes.

CHAPTER 13:
BALANCING WORK AND PARENTING

Single fathers who work less than full time: 10.2 %

Single mothers who work less than full time: 66. 2 %

Custodial fathers who receive a support award: 29.9 %

Custodial mothers who receive a support award: 79.9 %

Single fathers who work more than 44 hours per week; 24.5 %

Single mothers who work more than 44 hours per week: 7.0 %

Technical Analysis Paper No. 42,
U.S. Department of Health and Human Services, Office of
Income Security Policy, Oct. 1991, Authors: Meyer and
Garansky.

For many single parents it's a struggle to earn enough to pay the bills each month. Earning the money to pay for shelter, groceries, and the ever-increasing needs of maturing children can eat up more and more time. Still, divorced parents expect each other to do everything possible to financially and, at the same time, emotionally meet their children's needs.

Kids are great motivators. There may be nothing fathers love more than being viewed by their children as the loving provider. Whether their kids are living with them or not dads dread having to say, "Sorry, I just can't afford it."

Avoiding the Trap of Materialism

Another thing driving men to work long hours is materialism. For some, grand homes, exotic cars, glamorous women, comfortable retirement, and envious subordinates, provide an ego-pleasing sense of success. For such men, prosperity is often their only legacy.

Those who are preoccupied with the material risk having things instead of relationships as monuments to their fatherhood.

Groomed from birth to fill the provider role, men's self-esteem is often dependent on their ability to provide financially for their families. To the detriment of their children, fathers may choose to put all available time and energy into work in place of parenting.

Former spouses sometimes misconstrue men's drive to work as insensitivity to their children's needs. When it appears to a mother that earning money takes priority over the emotional needs of her children, that their father is intentionally denying them his company, then conflict is likely. First she feels sorry for her children, then she resents their father.

Michael B. is 50, a Vietnam veteran, who can, when he chooses to, work 60 hours a week. He describes himself as a longhair who makes a good living as a computer programmer. At 10:00 P.M. we are sipping black coffee in the bone-white living room of his sparsely furnished newly built condominium. Michael is pale and has dark rings under his eyes. He chooses his words carefully:

"Lately, I have been in some financial fear. Last month, I had a car wreck that set me back. And two weeks ago, I regressed into my financial insecurity again. That's where I think, 'I've got to work harder! I have to earn more! I must get caught-up right now! And that kind of thinking causes trouble between Dillon's mother and myself.

"When I overwork I feel guilty. And then I try to compensate by buying more for Dillon. Last week he was shopping with his mom and he saw a new Hot Wheels car, and he asked her to get it, and when she said, no, Dillon asked her 'What kind of a parent are you?' She came unglued on me because she thought I was competing with her for Dillon's affection. Buying his favor.

140

"It's real obvious when my focus changes from father to earner because Dillon changes. too. He gets moody. He's normally a very upbeat kid with lots of energy. Everyone is tickled to be around him. What happens when I work too much is Dillon withdraws. He loses his self-assuredness and starts acting shy. I want to help him feel good about himself. And I know that what makes children feel good about themselves is getting enough attention from both of their parents.

"Dillon's reaction to my overworking shows up more at Cass' house than at mine. When he's with me he acts like, 'I'm so glad to see you Dad.' But as soon as we're at his mom's house Dillon changes radically, and Cass sees it right away. She notices every change, from how his homework suffers to how he answers her questions. When Dillon's self-esteem is low Cass' workload doubles."

The Dangers of Making Work the Top Priority

When fathers make their work the top priority they set in motion a process with a predictable outcome. First, their children feel a sense of loss, which in turn makes the mother's life more difficult. Then, Mom begins thinking,

"If he wants to work so bad why doesn't he let me take care of our kids? Time with me would be less stressful. Why are they in childcare when I could be watching them? He ought to pay me instead. Then he could work all he wants."

For those who were force-fed the attitude of work first, materialism can seem to be a part of their being. Thinking back and in turn coming to grips with what one was taught about work as a child may make it easier to prioritize parenting and working. Michael's childhood experiences, explained below, are extreme, I think most men will relate in some degree to what he experienced as a child:

"As a kid I had this low self-worth. I didn't think much of myself. As I grew older my self-esteem started coming from my ability to work. Eventually, if I wasn't working I felt as if

141

I was doing something wrong. The idea that work is all-important was drummed into me. In a nutshell, I was taught that I had worth only when I produced."

For many, the pattern of long days at work led to their spouse's belief that the children are better off with her. Fathers can set in motion a downward spiral. For example, a wife feels resentful when her man does not pay attention to her or his children. If the lack of attention persists, the pair often divorces. If he in turn does not visit his children regularly she may decide not to honor the father's relationship to his children.

Julie is 32 years of age. She is a second-generation New Yorker who moved to California to study music at UCSC. Her son William is 10 years of age. He seldom leaves his mother's side. Ten years ago the two of them moved to California, where she remarried and completed her master's program in music theory.

She summed up William's relationship with his father this way.

"Sure, Stewart is a good provider but, if he had put one half of the energy into his son that he expends everyday at the office everyone would have been happier. When William and I separated I was willing to stay in the New York area so that Stewart could have a relationship with his father. But when William chose work over his own son time and time again I decided to start anew in California."

Putting Children's Needs First

The decision to parent more and work less is seldom easy. Surrendering their financial ambitions to satisfy children's emotional needs requires men to change some basic beliefs and measures of self-worth. Fortunately, many mothers prefer men who are good fathers to those who are great providers. Most men making the change to involved parenting find that they need the encouragement and help of friends and family if they are to avoid the old pattern of working sixty-hour weeks and spending a few hours with their children.

Fathers who ask family and friends to assist them in being more involved parents may find themselves deluged with invitations to participate in outings and holidays. Experiences of that kind may serve as gentle reminders that many of life's pleasures feel better than the sense of success that fathers get from earning money. Without the assistance of friends and family many men fall back into familiar roles, and when the old work patterns reoccur even the best co-parenting arrangements begin to break down.

Limiting the number of hours at the office can cause tension with fellow employees who work full time. People who choose to work fewer than forty hours per week appear to some to be in conflict with what corporate America values most, dedication to the job, at times to the exclusion of everything else. Fathers who limit their on-the-job hours are generally valued less as employees than men who do not co-parent.

Tim Hartnett is a devoted father, Marriage Family Child Counselor and the author of "Daddy Man" a regular column in *Growing Up In Santa Cruz*, a weekly newspaper that caters to parents of young children. His office is twenty minutes from the heart of California's Silicon Valley and for more than a decade he has counseled hard-working mothers and fathers who find themselves pressed to work 60 hours and more each week:"In the corporate world you risk being regarded as unmotivated. Unless you're going up you're going down. In Silicon Valley there is not much support for people who say, 'Look, I'm happy in this job, I'm going to stay here until my kids are raised.' If you are not going for the promotion, you are going to be replaced."

Working Less Is Scary, But Can Be Very Rewarding

Co-parenting individuals don't want to be laid off and passed up for promotions. Many are already financially strapped. The consequences of turning down work — being fired — is especially frightening to parents who must live on meager budgets. Many are painfully aware that they and their children are only a paycheck away from homelessness.

Making matters more stressful, it appears that in the future, there may be fewer social programs available to help families in financial trouble. For example, the 1997 Welfare Reform Legislation imposed stricter limits on those receiving state and federal financial assistance.

At the same time, when at job interviews single parents often find themselves competing with a line of people who are eager to work sixty-hour weeks. Almost all co-parents can use the money that a full week's work generates, yet many, in order to better parent, choose to work a modified schedule or part time.

Sipping coffee at Denny's Restaurant during his lunch hour, Tom C., a single father of two for the past 11 years, explains how he handles the work versus parenting dilemma.

"Generally, I didn't get a lot of respect from men who commuted to work or who worked long days. They thought I should be out working forty hours a week, like they did. It's that old macho thing, but I was really happy doing what I did, working part-time as a city parking attendant, and raising my kids. Maybe the guys didn't understand my reasoning.

"The Joe that works for somebody else is working a standard forty-hour week. The guy who has his own business is probably putting in sixty or seventy hours. Sure, they will buy their kids bicycles, roller blades, hockey sticks, mopeds and cars.

"At the same time those fathers who are working sixty hours per week are missing their kids' childhood. That saddens me and that is exactly what I was not willing to do.

"I worked part-time for five years and we managed to get by. About half a year into it I lost the fear that we wouldn't have enough money. It dawned on me one day that we had enough money to live on, plenty of time to enjoy ourselves, and my kids weren't latch-key kids. That was all I needed."

Today, Ryan is 15 and Sara is 13. After school both attend dance and acting classes. They need less of their dad's supervision now than they did when they were younger and spent little time at school. Since Tom is needed less at home he recently moved on to a full-time position as a building inspector.

"I would encourage any father to consider working less, especially if his children are under ten years of age. When they are little they want you to be home when school is out. They look forward to a hug and time with dad. As kids grow more independent, like when a teenager's friends become all important to them, then parents can work more. It's pretty simple."

When ex-wives hear that fathers will be working fewer than forty hours per week, most become alarmed that their support payments will be reduced. Former spouses need to be reassured that fathers (a) intend to continue to assist financially, (b) intend to be physically present when the children are young and need two parents the most and (c) understand that working less creates a hardship for some mothers. Diplomacy from father to mother can do a lot in terms of limiting conflict between parents and avoiding trips to courts.

When frightened, some women may call the Family Law Division or District Attorney (DA) hoping to maintain the previous level of support. Unfortunately, those in the DA's office are not in the "cooperative parenting" business. While many of their staff understand and support the idea of shared parenting, their primary job is to collect child-support. When an Assistant DA. becomes involved, the parent's relationship can deteriorate.

A co-parenting arrangement, built on cooperation between parents, falls apart when a law enforcement agency is ushered in and in turn demands that dad pay up. Typically, the visiting father system is reinstated. Mom again tries to raise the kids alone. And the judge, mom's lawyer and the DA. coerce dad into sending money even though it may mean less time with his children.

Because of the father's intention to provide more emotionally, the mother's desire to maintain her cash flow, and the DA's role as child-support enforcement agency, the children's peace of mind can be placed in jeopardy.

Changing the Child-Support Arrangements

Men who choose to work less in order to parent more must be sure that the change in time at work is made in a practical way. Working part-time, like all other facets of co-parenting, requires fathers to first think the process through. Easing into more involvement with the children and part-time work means that dads will walk a fine line. They must do what is best for the kids without unnerving their former spouses. Always explaining their goal — the intention to share in the job of raising their children — will reassure her that his intentions are honorable and that she will continue to receive financial support.

Child-support is based on the father's past income. When the courts are calculating child-support judges usually want to see dad's last three years' tax forms, pay stubs for the previous six months and a recent profit and loss statement. When a father starts earning less, it becomes harder for him to make his payments because the court ordered payment is not automatically lowered to match his income. It would be easier to work less and parent more if courts and the DA's office responded quickly to changes in a father's income.

Unfortunately, due to the amount of time that the legal process requires for modifications, typically six months to one year, many fathers who are working less in order to parent more appear to be behind in child-support.

When pre-existing support orders cannot be met because support payments do not accurately reflect the current income,

Dad may appear to be a deadbeat and that in turn causes judges and the DA's office to view well-intentioned men with contempt.

To prevent such misunderstandings, a father can qualify his decision by placing in his case folder a letter that states (a) his intention to maintain a cooperative relationship with his children's mother, (b) his income and expenses as well as the updated support amount, and (c) his commitment to fulfill child-support obligations.

When the District Attorney's Office gets involved in a financial dispute, any progress the father may have made towards working less and parenting more generally comes to a halt. As Judge Cottle noted earlier, "the District Attorney's Office can make parenting matters worse. "

According to Kimberly Mel, Assistant DA (ADA), Family Law Department: "The problem is that we have a small staff overseeing 12,000 cases that are complex, diverse and ever-changing. We are working with a computer program that lacks flexibility. It's hard for those in my office to respond to individuals requesting changes in support using the present system which is based only on past incomes not on a fathers desire to spend time with children."

Having (a) reassured the children's mother that dad is not avoiding his responsibilities as the other parent, (b) placed relevant financial information in the court folder, and (c) filed the required forms at the court house and received the court's approval, fathers are likely to:

- Remain current with support payments
- Avoid wage attachments, job search reports and lectures from the DA.
- Plus the additional ten percent interest penalty attached to child-support arrears
- Keep his drivers license, assets in the checking account, and remain free from jail.

147

Wanda, (not her real name), is an ADA in family law. She is Latina, in her mid-twenties, has waist-length black hair, and is sitting on a walnut bench outside of a family courtroom in a tiny Sierra Pacific community. I'm sharing the bench and overhear her with a divorced dad. She offered him this explanation for the $8,000 bill he had received for late charges on child support payments.

ADA: We do not have the staff it takes to help fathers prove they have paid their child-support All we know is what shows up on our computers. I'm sorry but you have to produce the records showing that you paid on these dates."

Father: "How can you bill me $8,000 now for being late on a payment I made ten years ago? Do you know that my youngest is twenty-three years old? I paid my last child-support payment more than five years ago when she turned 18 and you're just now billing me for a late charge? That can't be legal."

ADA: "Sorry there is nothing that I can do. You have to produce the records showing you paid. It is not our job to prove you paid your support payments."

Amazingly, this father was able to locate canceled checks that erased $5,000 worth of interest and penalties. His bookkeeping went back twelve years, not quite far enough to cover all the questioned payments, so he was ordered to pay three thousand dollars plus three years of interest, at 10%.

According to Wanda "The funds and interest reimburse California tax payers for money the mother needed when on welfare and the penalty portion helps pay the expenses in the district attorney's office."

Since lowering the number of hours that a father works can jeopardize both his parenting and position at work, then such a father must ask himself, "Is striving to spend more time with my children worth the risk?" It is, when the safety and comfort that a father's presence provides for his children outweighs the potential for conflict — then of course being available to his family is advisable. When worried, it is good

148

to remember that many single parents do change careers, every day.

Working Parents' Success Stories

More and more companies are accommodating single parents and realizing benefits from doing so. Owners, managers, and personnel departments are coming to see that they can count on these caring individuals. Divorced parents who are jointly responsible for their children are typically dependable, hard-working adults who are anchored by family to their communities. The same personality traits found in devoted parents, love and commitment, are benefits to companies. Many companies are willing to negotiate creative work schedules that allow for shared parenting.

Cathy cares for Nathan, her twelve-year-old son, 26 days of each month. She works for a Silicon Valley company, and is a Management Information Systems Manager. She owns a condo in an upscale community that is a ten-minutes drive from her office. At a busy outdoor bistro, just three blocks from her home, she matter-of-factly explains her relationship with work and with her employer.

"I don't catch flack when I come in at 8:30 in the morning. Almost everyone else starts at 7:30, but I have to drop Nathan off at school first so I arrive later than most. I've never encountered a problem because of that. I leave early for doctor's appointments when I need to and it is acceptable. Of course I make sure that my work gets done. Sometimes I come in on weekends or stay late, whatever it takes. I love this company because they have worked with me. I've given a lot to them and they've given a lot back. I appreciate their flexibility and make sure that it is rewarded."

Even many of the "macho" building trades are making room for moms and dads. Troy is a recently divorced, thirty-five year old contractor. The father of two girls and a boy, he is tanned, trim, casual. His general contracting company employs thirty hard-working carpenters. A second-generation builder, like his father, Troy too is divorced and raising children while managing a company. "I understand how important it is for fathers to use up every minute of visitation time with their children. So, I allow the guys to leave the job early on Fridays and show up late on Monday if that is necessary to get their kids to school. I know visitation time is limited and that there is plenty of time in the week to make up for hours spent with kids."

It is becoming more common place for businesses to support their employed parents. Single fathers who need to adjust their work schedules in order to fulfill their children's needs can feel confident. With adequate planning, devoted dads are designing and implementing schedules that meet both the needs of their company and family. When child-care is blended into the work and parenting equation, co-parenting just becomes that much easier for those who wish to parent more and work less.

How to Go About Changing Your Working Schedule

Here is a checklist to refer to when drawing up new, or refining existing, work schedules:

1. How many hours can I work on parenting days?
    4   6   8

2. Can I put in extra time on non-parenting days?
    6   8   10

3. Is working four, or three, ten hour days a possibility?
    yes   no   unsure

4. Can I work productively at home on parenting days?
    yes   no   unsure

5. Is my boss open to modifying my schedule?
    yes   no   unsure

6. Does my parenting plan interfere with company goals?
    yes   no   unsure

7. Shown on a calendar is my plan easily understandable?
    yes   no   unsure

8. Have I verbalized my proposed schedule to a friend?
   yes   no   not yet

9. Can I articulate my ideas concisely and confidently?
   yes   no   not yet

10. Am I willing to listen to and research alternative ideas?
    yes   no   unsure

11. If they   say no can I accept the rejection graciously?
    yes   no   unsure

Armed with a well-thought-out plan, one that takes into account his responsibilities at work and allows for co-parenting, a father can now consider when, where and to whom to make his request.

- Timing is important: Talk with the boss when he can give you his full attention.

- Tailor the meeting to suit the management: Some managers prefer to discuss possible changes over business lunches. Others, especially those concerned with the employee's privacy, prefer to meet in the safety of their own offices. Suggest a setting where management is apt to feel relaxed enough to discuss *all* possible working schedules.

- Dress appropriately for your presentation: Do all you can to present yourself as an employee worth keeping.

- Speak assertively: Explain what you have in mind, stress the benefits to the company with sincerity and conviction. Avoid emotional pleas. Remain professional.

Men who survive the divorce process and move forward to create co-parenting arrangements can draw strength from having weathered some of life's most stressful challenges. As a result such fathers can afford to feel confident. After all, they have the skills necessary to persuade a an employer to accommodate single parenting. Those who experience self-doubt may want to renew their spirits by remembering how far they have progressed since their marriage first broke up, remembering that in the beginning many were allowed only two or four hour visits once or twice a week. Back then the future seemed very bleak. Now for many life has never been better, and hints at still more time with their children in the days ahead.

CHAPTER 14: DATING IN CO-PARENTED FAMILIES

To fear love is to fear life, and those who fear life are already three parts dead.

Lord Russell (1872-1970)

Most divorced dads will again crave the attention of a lover. The need for a romantic evening seems to be inevitable, especially for the young at heart who have finished grieving the loss of a marriage. When done responsibly, the seeking of companionship need not cause problems for co-parents or their children. Those who get in trouble generally have either aroused jealousy in their former mate or in some way have put their children at risk.

Seeking companionship or romance is not a problem for co-parents when done responsibly. Ideally divorced parents will discuss, before either begins the search for a new lover, how to handle the introduction of new loves into the family. Fears can be managed by talking in advance about limiting the children's exposure to their parents' love interests. Such a discussion is personally challenging and timing is important. For example it would be foolish to discuss dating with a former lover who still hurts from being abandoned.

Write a Letter

To some the idea of discussing future dating with their children's mother is scary. They think what if she freaks out, gets jealous or hateful, and takes me to court? She could take my children away from me. It is certainly wise to consider how the children's mother might react. A jealous person can do a lot of damage to a family. At the same time it is best if fear does not stand in the way of necessary discussion. A well-thought-out talk can do much to eliminate jealously. One way to lessen the impact and to demonstrate respect is to make the announcement in a short letter. Correspondence affords the parents the opportunity to communicate early in the dating process. A note of intent can be both an example of respect for the former spouse's feelings and a demonstration of dad's commitment to shared parenting.

An example might look like this:

Hello _____.

I hope all is well with you. Things are fine on this end, still committed to working with you to raise the best of children.

Can we discuss a matter that is important to me? I want to find a companion and plan to start dating soon. Rest assured this will be a slow and responsible process. The children will not be introduced to a string of acquaintances. As you know in their eyes you are the best mother in the world. I reinforce that at every opportunity.

After considering their feelings and after much introspection I believe I can date without disturbing them. All dating will occur when the kids are with you and there will be no overnight visitors when the children are at my home. Anyone I find interesting will be screened to eliminate those who may be incapable of fitting into our family. If I find someone who I believe may fit, you and the kids will meet her. How you feel about a potential companion of mine matters. If you have a concern about anyone I spend time with please share your thoughts with me. Feel free to respond with a letter.

Regards, _____

Honest and considerate correspondence shows respect for the ex-wife's feelings and an intention to protect the emotions of those in the family. Still the letter may be received differently depending on the former mate's emotional condition. A divorced person who has moved on with her life will accept a letter of intent graciously. The former spouse who is emotionally attached to her ex is likely to feel threatened. The men who left their children's mother and now intend to date may want to think long and hard about how their letter may make the children's mother feel. There will be situations where discretion is needed. Time is a great healer and it may be wiser to mail a letter later rather than soon. While the mother may not share her past mate's desire for a new lover, a show of concern by him models consideration and his kindhearted approach has potential to improve their parenting relationship.

There will be opportunities for single fathers to date. This was Dan and Renny's fate.

"I had just finished my Masters Degree when I met Dan. He was teaching at San Jose State until he got a job offer at UC Santa Cruz; I wanted to take over the position he was leaving. I met with the department chair and with Dan, then he and I ended up talking in the hall. I pursued him because he thought I was too young. Dan was over forty and I was twenty-nine when we met."

Ambitious men have ample opportunity to date. Well-thought-out shared parenting does not limit people; instead it allows for fuller lives. Dads can go dancing or to the movies when the kids are secure at their mother's. The opportunity for single people to raise children, work and play is another advantage to co-parenting. It is easy to parent one week and date the next. For most single fathers dating is not a problem, but there are certain rules that deserve respect.

It is important that during the first year both parents date only when the children are at the other home. Men who invite dates over too soon after their divorce are being insensitive to their kid's feelings.

Children are extremely loyal to their parents and to their past marriage. Sometimes, years after the divorce kids still hope mom and dad will get back together.

One father, Raymond, a commercial refrigeration contractor had this experience: "Eight months after my divorce I walked into my bedroom and found Jessie, he was five years old, standing on my dresser trying with all his might to rehang his mother's and my wedding picture. He was crying. It broke my heart seeing him try to rehang the picture of his mom and dad."

Let Your Kids Set the Pace

When new people are introduced to kids they may not be welcomed. Many parents do not realize that for their kids no one can ever take the place of the other parent. While replacing his children's mother may not have been the father's intention, the presence of another woman is often enough to trigger a child's sense of loyalty to mom and in turn defiance of father. Dads cannot force their children to accept someone new. Men save themselves, their children and new friends a great deal of embarrassment by going slow.

"Dan brought me to his home specifically to meet Deirdre. He ran all his potential girlfriends by his daughter to see how she liked them. If Deirdre hadn't liked me, he wouldn't have pursued our relationship. It mattered a great deal to him that everyone was compatible."

The children's interest in the new person should be used to set the pace for future meetings. As the children warm up, increase their contact with your love interest. Renny, Dan's second wife, tells of her experience with Dan's daughter: "The second or third time I saw Deirdre, she gave me one of her high school pictures. I didn't think that much about it at the time, but Dan said that was a major gesture of acceptance on her part."

It's a Complicated Situation

Dating a single parent is more complicated than going out with someone who does not have children and an ex-wife. Patience and caution will pay off. Here are a few points to consider:

- Many women do not understand how challenging it is to date men with children. It will take them months to fully realize the dynamics necessary to fit into the family. Dealing with a combative ex-wife is reason enough for many girlfriends to leave a relationship.

- Few women are prepared for the realization that the children's needs come before their own. Girlfriends come and go but a conscientious father's number-one commitment is always his kids.

- It takes most women a year or more to discover whether or not they are capable of step-parenting throughout the child's life. Patience from the single fathers allows women time to decide if shared parenting works for them.

- And now, from the man's perspective. Here an ounce of prevention is worth a pound of cure. Fathers are patient when dating because:

- Since children are dad's first priority, and raising kids is time-consuming, it will take a father longer to move through the dating process than it does a man without kids. Fathers simply have fewer hours to spend with the women of their dreams than bachelors do.

- Single dads are busy people and many discover after dating a while that "working on their relationship" is not high enough on their list of priorities to satisfy a girlfriend — children simply come first.

- Some discover that spending time with kids is simpler and more fun than dating. This is especially true in relationships with women who need large blocks of "quality time" with their mate in order to feel loved.

- Fathers who believe a casual relationship with a woman will lessen their parenting load are mistaken. Parenting time and responsibilities increase as children age, and the older kids are the more they want to do. Ask the guardian of a fourteen-year-old how much time he or she has for dating and the answer will probably be little or none.

Dan met Renny a year after his divorce. He was fortunate. They married and spent years together. Some dads spend years looking before they find a compatible mate.

Tom has full physical and legal custody of his two children. His ex-wife, Shannon, generally visits her kids on the weekends. Tom says: "I hear women say all the time, 'Men never want to date a woman who has kids.' Well, let me tell you, for every one man that does not want to date a woman with children, there are ten women that don't want to date a man with kids. I think it is because women can bear their own children and some just don't want to raise other people's kids. With every woman I have dated, the fact that my kids aren't hers has become an issue. Especially when she wants to have more and I don't."

It's the father's responsibility to protect his children's emotions. Understanding a prospective love's wants and desires before introducing her to his family allows him to screen out women who clash with his family's needs.

Good co-parenting requires fathers to date as few women as possible. Men who limit the number of girlfriends they introduce to their ex-wives and children will have happier families.

Danny has a 10-year-old daughter and a son who is 12. He enjoys tailored sports coats, the best Italian shoes and his own wit: "Most of the women I date already know about my family. If not, I tell them right off. The conversation goes like this. 'I'm a single dad with two kids. If you and I have a relationship, you have one with my kids too. We're a package and with a lot to offer.' I'll be jovial when talking to her about a possible relationship between her and me but I'll make sure she understands I am completely committed to my kids. If she is mature she'll respect me for having that attitude and accept the limits my devotion to my family places on her relationship with me."

Time allows a man the opportunity to feel confident that his girlfriend can make a positive contribution to his children's lives. If she is not a good role model for their education, career, or relationships the children need to be shielded from her so they do not have the opportunity to become emotionally attached.

Referring back to Renny as an example: "I believe that all parenting is elective. Where I got to know Deirdre I wanted a relationship with her. Whether you're biologically related to your child or not, you choose whether you want to parent a child."

Questions to Ask When Dating

Here are some practical questions fathers can research:

- Does she want to have children of her own? If she does, will that work with your plans for the future?

- Is she financially self-sufficient? Most single fathers don't have extra money; if they do the children deserve the lion's share.

- Does she want to help with the parenting? If not, a request from the father will lead to resentment.

- Was she abused as a child? Not all abused children grow up to be abusers, but some do. If she was abused and she's around your children her past feeling will surface and your family will have to deal with her issues. Fathers have every right to ask, with respect and kindness, about their prospective mate's past.

It is equally important that fathers ask themselves questions, like:

- Do I want to marry again? If not the woman needs to be told immediately before she or the children are emotionally hurt.

- Am I only physically attracted to this person? Children can be shielded from relationships that will end when the lust dies down.

- Am I placing my family's wellbeing before my desire to find a companion? If not, can I expect my co-parenting to last?

- Do I have any issues such as emotional, sexual or physical abuse that need to be addressed before attempting another relationship? Do I have reason to expect my next relationship to be better than my past marriage?

Children with divorced parents are in a precarious position. If both mom and dad are dating the odds are high that children's hearts will again be broken by a loved one leaving. Their hope is that the parents will go slow when dating, and be discerning of those they meet.

Of course there are no guarantees that a relationship will last — a truth that children with divorced parents know too well. Because of the sense of loss that kids feel when loved ones leave their life, it is ludicrous to ask them to accept more than a few women into their families. If the father wants to be respected as a parent he needs do everything within his power to guarantee that the people he invites into the family have a sincere desire to remain. The more selective a father is the less risk there is for his children that a woman they love will simply move on and out of their lives.

> "Deirdre and I made a separate commitment to each other. I said I was going to be her stepmother and she was going to be my stepdaughter and that was independent of my relationship with her dad. And nine years later that turned out to be true when Dan and I divorced. One of the first things I did was make a trip to see Deirdre, she was living in L.A., to assure her that I wasn't leaving her. It has been a year and a half now and everything has been fine between Deirdre and me."

At the very least, when a long-term relationship fails a father can ask his former girlfriend to maintain her friendship with his children. Then he can do everything in his power to help her maintain their relationship.

The fact that children do bond quickly with people creates problems. Generally it takes adults longer to commit to each other than it does for kids to open their hearts to strangers. After only a few meetings with an acquaintance, children can be asking, "Daddy, is Susan your girlfriend? Can she stay for dinner? Can she spend the night?" One way to temper the children's enthusiasm is to remind them that Susan is a friend who has her own home and life to look after. Fathers can refer to prospective mates as friends until they feel certain both adults are committed and that their relationship will in turn be long lived.

As a friend, when she visits she's welcome to socialize. Hopefully everyone will interact and enjoy each other's company. As the family grows accustomed to her, she and the father begin to discuss boundaries. For instance her relationship with the kid's dad will be best served if:

- She aligns herself with the father, thus supporting his position as the primary parent.

- She avoids taking the children's side in arguments and never debates the father in front of his kids. If she attempts to get acceptance from the children by supporting their causes she jeopardizes her relationship with the father, as well as his relationship with his children, by undermining his authority.

- She relates to the children as an adult to a child, never as their peer. If her relationship with the father moves past dating she will want the children to treat her as an adult.

Looking Out for the Kids at Mom's House, Too

Fathers have the right to look out for their children's feelings even when the kids are at mom's house. All of the screening and boundaries that fathers practice applies to their ex-wives. Mothers too must practice discretion when dating.

Inappropriate forms of adult play at mom's house needs to be addressed. The most common unacceptable practice is sleeping with a new boyfriend while the kids are home, especially during the first year. Most judges frown on this. They know that parents sleeping with people other than the kid's biological parent is upsetting and can emotionally damage children.

When a father becomes aware that his ex-wife's relationship with her new boyfriend is emotionally hurting his kids, he needs to take action. Most men do feel afraid. They will not want to upset the ex-wife. Once again dad thinks, "If I make her mad she'll take the kids away from me."

Despite this fear most men take action. Allowing unhealthy situations to exist creates more resentment than addressing poor behavior. The ex-wife might at first be angry, but eventually she may respect him for having the courage to address a situation that was harmful. Of course fathers must always practice good judgment when confronting ex-wives. Discussing questionable situations with knowledgeable friends before taking action is a must.

Within the first year an ex-husband can often persuade his ex-wife to stop sleeping with lovers in her home when the kids are there. A respectful letter stating his concern that their children will be emotionally hurt might do the trick. If that does not work a man can bring her behavior to the attention of their Special Master, custody counselor, or judge. It is almost certain that an inappropriately sexually active ex-wife will be told to cool her libido until the children are at dad's house.

Sometimes the insistence of a father that his former spouse curtail her dating when their children are present works to increase his time with the kids. An example, when a divorced woman has her children every day of the month except for two weekends she soon realizes that the schedule limits her sex life.

If she is approached by the father in a considerate manner with an offer to watch the children when she wants to date, she may accept the father's offer to watch their children. If this works out, in a few months when the timing feels right, the father may negotiate a change in the parenting schedule.

Avoiding Jealousy

Few emotions cause more embarrassment or damage than jealously. After co-parenting on a fifty-fifty basis for eight years, John attended his first support group. In the Divorced Fathers Network meeting he shared the following:

> "I had a great relationship with my ex-wife until I remarried. Immediately after the wedding I was served with papers saying she wanted custody of our children. The next week, when it was time for me to watch them she refused to bring them home. When I phoned her she told me to get a lawyer. After eight years of cooperation now she wants full custody.
>
> "When we went to court I told the judge I didn't want a custody battle and I was not going to give up on my kids. He respected me for my attitude and ordered Barbara and I into custody counseling."

Whenever possible, a father avoids situations where the former-spouse may feel tormented. Granted, it is not possible to insulate her from every situation that might make her uncomfortable, and that is not a father's job. Still, problems can be avoided by consciously considering her feelings.

Jealously causes problems most commonly when one person appears to be replacing the other. This can be as blatant as hearing his daughter tell of mom introducing Hector as the new daddy. Or as indirect as the mother overhearing her children arguing saying something as silly as, "Daddy's girlfriend loves me more than you. She plays with me more than mommy plays with you." Often jealously leads to resentments that can flare into battles.

Recognizing potentially difficult situations and then treading lightly does much to ease the pain of jealousy. Renny, Deirdre's stepmother, supplies an example:

> "Dan, Mickie and I had a conference about Deirdre's financial aid application for college. That is potentially difficult, but this was a time when we pooled our resources effectively. Dan and Mickie brought their tax returns and we all sat around the table. I did the filling out of forms because I had recently been a graduate student myself.

"One of the things that really bothered Dan was that we had to decide for purposes of financial aid who was the custodial parent. The college Deirdre went to had the Divorced Parent's Statement. Dan hated that form because we chose Mickie as the custodial parent and Dan the divorced parent. Mickie made less money so that heightened Deirdre's eligibility for financial aid. Those were very cold-hearted decisions that we made together so Deirdre could attend a very expensive university. That was just one legal area where we ran into a setup where someone's jealously could have been triggered."

The easiest way to remain secure is to remember that no one ever takes the place of dedicated parents. Those who are involved in their children's lives can rest secure in the knowledge that their children love them. No one can take the place of a loving parent.

Problems with Using Stepparents as Mediators

One pitfall co-parents make is to place a step-parent in the position of mediator; the divorced couple converse via this "neutral" person. There are major problems with using step parents as go-betweens.

Gail has been struggling in her co-parenting relationship with Les for nine years. He married his second wife, Alise, six years ago. She became the stepmother to Marisa and trouble began. Gail recalls it starting this way:

"One afternoon, Alise came up to me and said Les told her to handle the visitation scheduling. Les hadn't said one word to me before hand. I was so angry and humiliated. Alise told me that from now on there would be only one phone number I could call to speak with Les. I was to leave a message on his answering machine, and after they had talked, Alise would get back to me. I wanted to be able to talk directly to Les about Marisa's school. Some things you have to discuss and process. Like how are we going to handle her homework or drama classes? Co-parenting can't be done on an answering machine. And it got weirder. After that Alise said to me, 'Gail, you have to be good to me because I'm the only one who will talk with you.' That statement filled me with anxiety.

"I won't communicate with him through his new wife anymore. I sent them a letter requesting private mediation. If they don't agree to voluntary mediation I'll get court-ordered mediation and Alise won't be allowed in, because only parents can talk in there."

There are huge pitfalls with using stepparents as go-betweens. Communication between the biological parents can break down. If one parent has not remarried and the other has, when the need arises for the child's mother and father to discuss parenting issues, the single parent can feel, or be, ganged up on by the married couple. Feeling outnumbered can limit a person's desire to work at problem solving. Stepparents who play the role of mediators deny their step-child's parents the opportunity to lean the skills needed to work together. The children in turn see their parents fail to learn the skills needed for harmonious shared parenting.

The willingness to communicate is what maintains co-parenting. Without continued dialogue between fathers and mothers there is little chance of ever creating mutual respect. One of the biggest benefits of co-parenting to children is the advantage of living in two homes with parents who have earned the admiration of each other.

Equality in parenting between couples starts when men insist on a balance of power in the family and the opportunity to share in the raising of their children. From that point, a healing begins. As sons witness their father's commitment to them, and to working with their mothers, boys learn to honor their own rights as parents. When daughters see their father's commitment to families, and the resulting benefits to all, girls learn the value of men. In the future sons and daughters may, for the good of their own children, demand equal involvement in their families.

CHAPTER 15: ENVISIONING THE FUTURE

Looking back, what I appreciate most about the way my
parents raised me is that my relationship with my dad is as
strong as the one I have with my mom. He was willing to be a
parent and she was willing to not have the money. I was
fortunate. A lot of kids don't get to be raised in families with
joint custody, even thought they love their dads.

Deirdre, age 24

The aim of most divorced fathers is to progress from
"fighting" — natural enough in the immediate aftermath of a
breakup — to the sort of cooperation that will benefit their
children, ex-spouses, and themselves. Even those who feel
bitter when they think about their ex-wives know, deep within
themselves, that harmony in the disrupted family is a worthy
pursuit.

If an ex-spouse misunderstands a father's intention and
sees no value in his continued involvement in his family, then
creating mutual respect won't be accomplished easily. There
are bound to be former spouses who will sabotage all attempts
to build a co-parenting relationship. After all, if an angry
spouse can destroy her former mate's desire to cooperate it
will serve her goal of having sole control of her children's
lives.

There is power to be gained by managing the children. In
family law control of the kids equates to power. Whoever
governs the little ones has the attention of the court.

The gender bias in family law makes mothers less
motivated to cooperate. Knowing they are favored allows
some to feel secure enough to manipulate the legal process,
further frustrating their ex-husbands. Numerous court
appearances, requests for psychiatric evaluations, false
allegations, and unnecessary restraining orders hinder
attempts by fathers to make peace.

In a contested custody case it is generally the father who brings the vision of family harmony to the table. He is most likely the one seeking parental equality. He is the one being denied. Christine Copeland, Family Law Facilitator, and a the guest speaker at the Santa Cruz, California, Divorced Fathers Network meeting, shared that seventy-five percent of those who use her service are men and most are fathers with parenting issues.

If a father is a persistent man who is serious about succeeding then he will have chosen for himself a situation to strive for — the model of shared parenting — one he believes is the best possible option for his family.

In spite of the obstacles they face, more and more divorced dads are creating arrangements where there is parity between themselves and their children's mother. Those who are successful are unanimous in stating that a father will most certainly have to:

- Defend his children's right to have two involved parents.

- Increase his communication skills and problem solving techniques.

- Rely on his peers to help him avoid mistakes and to sustain enthusiasm for the creation of the shared parenting arrangement that he believes best suits his family.

Three Categories of Divorced Parents

Divorced parents tend to fall into three categories.

There are the couples that are contentious, moms and dads who fight over every detail, exhibiting a complete lack of trust. These parents make up less than ten percent of divorces, yet they take up the lion's share of the court's resources. Restraining orders, verbal and physical abuse, false allegations, compulsive behavior and addiction, are common for such cases. To the observer it is obvious that it will require years of work to improve these relationships and that separating the parents is best.

Then there are the hesitant adults where tension stems largely from a particular painful event. Someone has been betrayed. One parent chose to leave. A heartfelt amends by one party and forgiveness from the other is needed to instill a sense of trust. Time must pass to allow for the healing of emotions. In the case of some parents, a larger problem such as fulfilling the needs of their children makes the past hurts irrelevant.

Finally, there are the families where parents divorce because they decide that splitting up is the best thing to do for their family. Mom and dad agree that they are not a match, yet they believe in each other as parents. These are adults who will be tested both by the financial challenge of creating two homes and by the feelings of loss that arise when she/he commits to share the days of their child's life.

Three Stories

What follows are three short interviews. Each provides a glimpse into what different people create for themselves, their kids, and the future. The parents in the first interview asked to be interviewed in their own homes. The second family, parents and daughter, decided to meet at the father's house. And the final interview, parents, step-parent, and daughter offered to conduct their interviews at my home. People were questioned one at a time. They were unable to hear or see each other when answering questions and sharing experiences. To efficiently cover topics, for comparison, and to ensure that the information flows smoothly, I have grouped the related comments of the second and third families. For example, Mickie's, Dan's, Deirdre's and Renny's comments are interwoven even though they occurred on various days. The integrity of each person's words and meaning are maintained.

The first couple, Allen and Karen, are having a tough time sharing their two children. The parents divorced six years ago and they have been in the family law system ever since; there have been dozens of court appearances.

The second pair, Alex and Jean, divorced ten years ago. They have managed to co-parent their daughter through those years despite decisions made early on that placed the mother in financial debt.

Mickie and Dan divorced nineteen years ago and co-parented for 12 years. Two years ago, they witnessed their daughter, Deirdre, graduate from M.I.T. and recently they attended her wedding, confident that she was both emotionally prepared for marriage and the raising of children.

Allen and Karen

Allen and Karen were married in 1983, separated in 1990, and six months later were officially divorced. They have two children, Alice and Kyle, ages 12 and 8.

Leaning back in her swivel chair, Karen is verbose, unblinking, disarming. When she speaks there is a controlled, persuasive, almost pleading tone. Her emerald eyes are wet, her almond hair cut full and round frames a youthful face punctuated with rose red lipstick. Her sky blue silk blouse and pin-striped pants are professionally pressed, and the creasing accentuates her height. She looks and sounds committed to convincing all that she is the person capable of shattering all glass ceilings.

Her interview takes place downstairs in the home office. A new PC sits center stage on a tidy oak desk. Her home is half a block from a cluster of beige concrete county buildings where fiberglass fishing boats on rusting trailers are parked at the curb. The house is quiet, the kids are with their father this week. A year after she and Allen divorced, Karen went off AFDC. Welfare reform occurred and for the past two years she has been attending college learning the skills she felt were necessary for a successful, home-operated advertising/marketing business. Her "list of clients is growing" and she is "making ends meet."

Question: Karen, what was it like when you first separated?

"The separation went well in the beginning. People declared that Allen and I had this insane relationship and the judge listened. I had almost full custody for the first year. I expected the court to see Allen as this volatile, dangerous person, and to keep him away from the kids, but the judge didn't do that. Now, Allen has joint custody."

Question: Has your relationship with Allen improved?

"I'd love to co-parent. I would love it. But the bottom line is this — Allen is not somebody I could stay married to, or even someone I can communicate with, so co-parenting, as far as I'm concerned, is not an option for us. With restraining orders I can keep Allen from calling or coming over."

Question: Have you felt supported by the community?

"Actually, I find there's a tremendous amount of support. There's the Parent Center, Women's Crisis Center, paralegal, attorneys that work on sliding scale, hot lines, AFDC . There's a lot of resources."

Question: Karen, how have your children handled your divorce?

"They are worse off today than six years ago. They're raging and emotional. They're very hard to control. I think they're really confused. They're scared of going back to Allen, but they want to go back, yet after visiting him they come here and fall apart. They seem to be wonderful when they're with him. When they are with me there is a lot of crying and falling apart. I don't understand it."

Question: What do you think it would take to improve your relationship with Allen?

"I wish I knew. All I know is that I'm not willing to work with him….. I don't know what to do. That's why I think there should be people with psychology backgrounds involved in divorce. They could help people deal with these situations."

Question: Regarding co-parenting do you have any plans for the future?

" I'm working with a lawyer and I'm not at liberty to talk about that."

Allen lives five miles from Karen, his former wife, ten minutes down the highway towards the Pacific Ocean. His house sits on the side of a sandy hill at the base of the Coast Range. There is a view of the neighbor's place one street below. Allen considers himself a Californian transplanted from Pennsylvania. He is six feet tall, trim, and wares his chestnut, shoulder-length hair tied in a pony tail. It hangs half way down the back of a starched short sleeved cotton shirt. Dark blue boot cut Levis cover well-worn lizard skin saddle shoes. As we walk through the house and into the kitchen, I'm offered coffee and lunch.

We sit at a scarred rectangular kitchen table. There is a view of the living room, double glass sliders and the sun-bleached deck outside. Sounds of kids flows through the wall. Allowing for his rambunctious children is a living room with a minimum of formal furniture. Instead, a waist high yellow rubber ball made for riding, complete with handle, rests in the corner. A wall of bookshelves filled with video boxes is interrupted by a fireplace. In the opposite end of the living room on a cluttered oak desk rests a tired Macintosh and a pile of manuscripts. How can I help you he asks and we begin.

Question: Allen, what was the process you used to establish yourself as a co-parent?

"The court. In the last four months Karen and I have been to court twelve times. During our divorce proceedings we went more than that. We made six appearances before I got as much time with the kids as Karen. We've been to court maybe thirty times. When the court knows the facts, I win. The kids win, definitely. It's when the judges don't have all the facts, that I'm at a disadvantage."

Question: Have you felt supported in your efforts to co-parent?

"No, I don't feel supported. There are some friends who understand and there are some counselors who aren't biased towards women, but other than that I have not been supported."

Question: Karen mentioned that the children are stressed. It so, how does that affect your relationship with her?

"Three months ago, the kids were out of control, they wouldn't stop fighting. I warned them, I slapped them both, just once on the butt. Karen freaked out. She said I couldn't see the kids again and had her attorney write a letter saying that I had physically hurt Alice. They sent copies to the sheriff, the judge, and C.P.S. The letter also said that Alice wanted to be the one who decides when she wants to see me. The very next day Alice started calling wanting to come back home. She called five times, but Karen wouldn't let her come over.

"Two weeks ago, Kyle called C.P.S. on his mother. Karen had grabbed him by the arm and dug her nails in. I saw his arm. Karen had definitely dug her nails in. Before I would have said, I'll talk to your mom, but not now. I'm not going to let her get away with anything now."

Question: Allen, what are you going to do next?

"I want her ordered into ongoing counseling and I'm working on having a judge order her to do that. The plan is to show the court what she's doing. What she is trying to do is make sure there is no contact between us as parents. If she puts that together, then, I think she believes the custody counselor will say, Since there's no communication between the parents, they can't co-parent. So, we're gonna let one be the primary caregiver. If Karen sets that up — I just hope the caregiver will be me."

I did not interview Alice and Kyle because of their ages. Fortunately, the court ordered their parents and the children to attend a six week program called "Kids Connection," a branch of Creative Family Connections, Inc. The entire family will receive some counseling. Hopefully the parents see the advantages of cooperation and learn how to "de-escalate" the fighting.

If not, maybe their children will learn how to protect themselves emotionally, either through peer and professional counseling, or by setting boundaries such as reminding mom and dad that children should not be included in parenting problems.

Summary: Allen and Karen are still in the combative stage of divorce. Neither has taken the initiative to acquire the skills necessary to make the transition into cooperation. Five years after the interviews both continue to place their futures in the court's hands. They have hired a Special Master to control their lives. No communication is allowed between parents. All information pertaining to the children and their parents must go through the Special Master. Each month Karen and Allen are billed for her services. To date their inability to cooperate has cost them $100,000 in legal fees and the end of their parenting woes could be at least six years away. Their youngest child is thirteen years old. Many states require parents to be financially responsible for their children through the age of nineteen.

Since the hiring of a Special Master, the quality of the children's lives has improved. Their parents don't fight anymore, children are not used as go-betweens, and those changes have allowed the children a chance to relax.

The Special Master that Allen and Karen have hired prevents conflict and may in turn facilitate a change. At the least she is producing a cooling-off period. As time passes and the parents tire of paying for a referee, mom or dad may decide to try and improve their situation. If either parent sees the futility of conflict and strives whole-heartedly to put an end to the fighting positive things can happen.

Jean, Alex, and Louisa

Jean is an energetic five-foot-two, 125-pound, blond woman who spent her college years, the early seventies, in San Francisco. Today, she is a property manager living in a quiet neighborhood surrounded by white stucco houses built in the 1950's. Her back yard has a dozen fruit trees surrounding an old tile fountain. Jean has been divorced for ten years. Her daughter, Louisa, was five when Jean and Alex separated. At the time of this interview Louisa was moving from Mom's house into Dad's house. Jean's plan is to move in with her boyfriend and rent her house out to pay off of an old debt.

Alex, Jean's ex-husband, lives next door to his former wife. He is second generation Mexican-American in his late forties who works as an investigator for the County Public Defender's Office. He is soft spoken, 165 pounds and five foot eight. I arrive for our interview at 9:00 am Saturday. Jean introduces me to Alex as he comes up her front porch steps. He is wearing tan slacks and a white T-shirt. Alex has a blue basket under one arm. He is delivering Jean's and Louisa's laundry. He nods an acknowledgment to me, walks into her house, and drops off a basket of freshly folded clothing. As a family they have one washing machine and dryer. It is at Alex's house so he does most of the laundry.

Louisa is an excelling fourteen year old. Shiny brown hair hangs to the middle of her back. She plays basketball and soccer in high school. Nike cross trainers, blue jeans, and a Converse sweatshirt are the clothes of the day. She moves from the refrigerator to the table, and prepares a salad. Looking up, she says hi. Louisa wants to move to San Francisco because it's bigger and there's more people there.

Question: Jean, I'm impressed that you and your ex-husband live comfortably next door to each other. How did that come about?

"Well, it wasn't always this way. Our relationship was a mess when we first divorced. I moved out of the house that we owned at the time. I wanted to rent an apartment, but he insisted that I buy a condo. I felt it wasn't a good idea, but I let him steer my boat. It was disastrous for me financially, I couldn't pay the mortgage. I lost the condo and that added another layer of resentment and problems to our relationship."

Question: Jean, tell me more about the resentment.

"I ended up with nothing out of our marriage other than my daughter. My daughter is wonderful, but I felt like Alex' life had remained stable but my life ended up in turmoil. There were days when I would just call on the phone and scream. I didn't hate him, but I blamed him for the collapse of the marriage and in my eyes he deserved it."

Question: How long did the hostility last?

"A couple of years. It would build up. He would do little things that, to me, were disrespectful and I'd lose it."

Question: Alex how did you weather Jean's anger?

"I didn't anticipate that things were going to be easy and neither did she. When she lost the condo, I knew I was in for it. I'm one of the few people who ever lost money in real estate in California. That was hard on me and it was harder on Jean. So when she would call up and start yelling I would just let her go."

Question: Jean, so money was your main point of contention?

"My major fear was that on my income I wouldn't be able to support my daughter and that he would take her from me. It was a pretty scary thought."

Question: When did things change?

" One day Alex realized what was going on. He was actually very hurt when I told him I was afraid he would try and take Louisa from me. He told me he would never try and take Louisa from me. He wouldn't dream of it."

Question: Alex, what advice would you give to fathers trying to outlive their ex-wives' anger and fear?

"I got this from a therapist. My best advice is to treat your ex-wife like a client. Go out of your way to make it easier for her. I am not suggesting anyone be a martyr here, that doesn't work, but try to help out of self-interest, the consequence is that your life is going to be easier. You're benefiting because you can be with your kid. It seems cold, treating her like a client, and it is a hard thing to do because of all the emotional stuff that goes on. It takes a lot of effort. You have to let a lot of water go under the bridge."

Question: Alex, how do you maintain your relationship with Jean?

" I keep in mind that we're stuck with each other. There's a lot of times in life when you can just move on but this is not one of them."

Question: Louisa, what's it like being fourteen and having your parents live next door to each other?

"It's fun and it's kinda weird."

Question: What do you think of co-parenting?

" It is different. Like there were different rules in each house. My Mom bosses me a lot more than my Dad does. Mom's way of parenting is good in some ways but it's kind of annoying too. Still, the co-parenting thing is good because like if I get tired of one of my parents . . . I have another one."

Question: Do you think your friends whose parents are divorced and don't co-parent are as happy as you are?

"No. If their dads like left when they got divorced and visit sometimes. My friends are like sore about the whole thing."

Question: Do you think they get over it?

"Deep down I don't think they really get over it. But when you get older, you get stronger about it."

Question: Louisa, are you glad your parents do more than visit?

"Yeah, definitely. I don't think I could have gone through that, but other people do, I mean, if you have to like have a dad that visits I guess you adapt."

Summary: Alex and Jean weathered divorce and the difficult consequences caused by their decision to purchase a condo. Both parents remained committed to shared parenting long enough to discovered and overcome the root cause of their contention — Jean's fear that someone would take Louisa from her. They did the leg work necessary to keep their family intact. Both understood early on that separation and co-parenting were difficult processes. They sought counseling and brought what they learned back to the family. "Co-parenting is still sometimes difficult." Jean confides, "But overall I don't think it has ever been easier."

Mickie, Dan, Renny and Deirdre

Mickie and Dan married in 1971, divorced in 1978. They have one child, Deirdre, who is now twenty-five.

Mickie is a soft-spoken Southerner from Texas. In a lazy voice she savors the telling of her family's history. Her hair is light brown and wavy. It covers her shoulders and blends into a autumn colored cotton dress. Mickie is an only child, raised by her mother; she never met her father.

"When I was growing up there wasn't a man in our house," she recalls, "My mother earned all her own money. So I naturally grew up expecting to pay my own way."

Following her mother's example of self-sufficiency, Mickie went on to earn a Ph.D.. in Anthropology. She is in charge of data entry for Social Services in Santa Cruz, California.

Dan, her ex-husband, is a clean-shaven, fair-haired man from the original New England settlement. He stands five foot eight, weights one hundred sixty pounds. He was chipper, dressed in a sport shirt and khakis when we met. Dan teaches history for the University of California in Santa Cruz and according to Mickie, "he has an intellect that can drive nails." When he speaks of his family's past a tone of contentment is followed by a smile.

Deirdre, their daughter, is confident and animated. Her voice is peppered with slang that is endearing. She is attractive with her mother's brown hair and her father's aloofness. Her youth shows despite the cotton work shirt that covers the tops of her Levis. She recently graduated from MIT, with a degree in biology. Currently, Deirdre is doing lab research, looking for the proteins that interact with neurotransmitter transporters, at Cal Tech.

Question: Mickie, how did you and Dan manage a child and complete graduate school too?

"When Deirdre was born her father and I were full-time students and we taught to support our graduate studies, so we developed the habit of sharing our time. When one of us was taking care of Deirdre, the other would be working. We had to trade off. When Dan and I divorced we wanted to keep sharing Deirdre."

Question: How did the court respond to your idea of sharing Deirdre?

"When Dan and I first separated and began preparing to get divorced, we talked to the judge who was overseeing the preliminary work for us. He was very skeptical about our plan, which was to have joint custody and for each of us to parent our child exactly half the time."

Question: Exactly how did you prepare for divorce?

"We read books about doing your own divorce. There wasn't a lot of property to divide so we went to a local divorce service and for a small fee they helped us fill out the forms. We filed everything ourselves.

"When we took our paperwork in to the judge he said joint custody was a nice idea, but that he'd not seen many of the

178

people who had tried it succeed. To convince him we told him that to force one parent to be the custodial parent would be an alien pattern for us. It was something that we had never done, and changing our parenting pattern would be really disruptive for our child."

Question: Dan, how did you handle the people who disapproved of co-parenting?

"I wouldn't give two cents for those people's opinions about parenting. I mean if anybody had said to me that they thought it was weird that I was interested in raising my kid, I probably would have laughed at them. I would have thought there's one more stupid person"

Question: Mickie, how did you avoid the money issue?

"You know, I don't understand the reason for it. The idea is foreign to me. If I chose to care about his money, my husband would have to be my enemy. And he wasn't really. Dan didn't turn out to be the best marriage partner for me. He turned out to be the best father I could have imagined. The incompatibility in our marriage was detrimental to all three of us, but our parenting had very little wrong with it.

"Each of us knows that if we need something, if we are really in a bind, that we will help each other out. We have always shared the cost of everything exactly 50%, all the food, all the clothing, all the medical care. Both of us were simply 100% parents when our daughter was with us. We both worked really hard for everything we got and, yeah, sometimes we were really poor."

Question: Mickie, how difficult was the transition from divorce to co-parenting?

"The transition from marriage to co-parenting was difficult for all three of us. I would come to pick Deirdre up at day care after school, and my ex-husband would already be there saying good-bye to her. One time we both just sat on the steps out front and cried. It was painful to both of us."

179

Question: Were your friends supportive?

"Dan belonged to a community of a dozen or so old-fashioned, hippie-type people who were very loyal. When he and I got married we all vowed that we would always be there for each other, throughout our lives. And in a kind of sweet, old-fashioned way they kept that promise. Co-parenting kind of eliminates the need for friends to choose between parents."

Question: Dan, other than the judge presiding over your case, did you encounter any resistance to your co-parenting?

"Deirdre's preschool teacher came to us very concerned that our daughter wasn't showing any signs of stress in reaction to the divorce. She said 'Deirdre must be holding back and refusing to show her grief.' The teacher thought Deirdre was becoming neurotic. Deirdre's grades were fine, she was well adjusted, but the teacher was concerned. We took Deirdre out of that school and put her in another with a teacher who had no such expectations."

Question: Deirdre, do you think co-parenting is better than having a stay-at-home mom and a visiting father?

"When I think about how I was raised what comes to mind is how different my life is from most people I meet. A lot of people I meet at school are unhappy, even if their parents live together. Their parents don't seem to like each other. I've only met a few students who basically liked going home.

"My parents get along even though they are not married. And I can't remember them ever fighting about anything having to do with me. I'd call my mom and say I'd like to stay out all night and she'd say 'Sounds like a really bad idea, call your dad.' Like, I'd tell him the same and he'd say 'Sounds like a really bad idea.' It was totally hopeless. They had disagreements but they were unrelated to me. They felt really good about not encouraging me to hate one or the other. I'd say 'God it drives me crazy when she does this' and he'd say, 'Your mom is a really good person. You have to cut her some slack.'

"I don't know how much this applies to other people. Like for me it would have been so horrible to have had to live with only one of them. It would have been crazy-making because neither of them wanted to not be a parent."

Question: So it's been perfect?

"No. What made me unhappy was before their divorce they used to fight a lot. That's the hardest part. It makes you sad that they're not together but nothing is as bad as their fighting. The only thing that's missing with co-parenting is that you seldom get to share experiences with both parents, but considering it all, that is not much."

I interviewed Renny, Deirdre's stepmother, two days before she left for a summer wilderness vacation in Montana. Her long brown hair fell onto the front of a faded red plaid shirt and worn jeans molded to a fit frame, a testament to hours of hiking. Far from being a recluse, Renny's life, her limitations and successes, all were available for discussion. "I was born and raised in California. I come from a working-class family and I'm the first to go to college. I ended up with a Ph.D. in American Literature and now I'm a professor in the English Department a San Jose State College."

Question: Renny, was there always good communication between the parents?

"Some things worked best with Dan and Mickie, some things Dan and I did best, and sometimes Mickie and I were tops. There were times when she and I cut Dan out of the loop. He was usually mad at us when we did that."

Question: Deirdre, how did you feel when Renny joined the family?

"My step mom came as late as she possibly could have and still have me feel like she's one of my parents. I was 14. It was sort of weird getting used to someone else's parenting. I think it was weird for her too. At first she didn't know what to do. She was good at a lot stuff that mom and dad were really lame at. Like, my parents were overly protective. Renny, was like, 'Well you know she's pretty responsible. Maybe you should lighten up a little bit, guys.'"

Question: Renny do you have any ground rules that you would suggest for stepmothers or parents?

"Don't interfere with the father's connection with his children or even his ex-wife. Respect the relationships that existed before you. Trying to make a place for yourself at the expense of someone else's relationship can only cause problems and who wants to live in a troubled family."

Question: Relating to parenting someone else's child, what advice do you have for stepparents?

"I have come to believe through experience that all parenting is elective. You choose whether you want to be really involved with a child. I know of biological parents who have, in essence, abandoned their children. And some of the best relationships I know are step parent/step child relationships."

Question: Renny, are you glad you made that commitment to Deirdre?

"Sure I am. It was wonderful. Actually, the best day of my life happened with the whole family. I had finished my first novel. I gave it to Dan to read and he liked it. Then we gave it to Mickie to read. Mickie came over on her way to work because she couldn't wait to tell me how much she liked my book and that was thrilling. When I came home that night, we all had dinner together, and that was the first time I realized I was part of something larger than myself, their family."

Question: Dan, do you think today's fathers are as devoted as those in your generation?

"The men I know who have children are interested in parenting and are active parents, even the divorced ones. The next generation does seem to be doing better in terms of being active parents."

Question: How do you feel about your relationship with Deirdre now that she is grown?

182

"It's interesting and engaging to watch a child grow. Some people think that all you see in raising a child is your reflection. But a kid is about half what you put in and half what they bring to the world. There are big parts of them that are not in any way like either of their parents.

"For me, the reward of parenting is this young adult, that knows more than you do about some things. I've been interested in biology and evolution for years. I don't know very much about it. I'll read something in the newspaper about biology and I'll phone her and she always knows more about it than what's in the newspapers. That's fun. You feel like you've really succeeded.

"It never stops either. I'm looking forward to grandchildren. She and her fiancé are talking about kids. She checked it out with the people at the lab. They said don't wait till the end of grad school. You don't want to start a career with an infant. Have your baby when you are out of the lab, during your last two years of grad school, when you are still at home writing your thesis. She really checked it out and that's fun to see."

Summary: Since children learn much from their parent's examples Deirdre's success in life is to some degree the result of her parent's choices. Their respect for each other, self-sufficiency, and ability to make their daughter's happiness a priority allows Deirdre to focus on her own life. Her parent's model of cooperation protects her belief in marriage and allows her to look forward to a partnership despite the experience of being raised by divorced parents. The mother's and father's respect for each other's right to parent meant that family friends did not have to choose sides and Deirdre could enjoy their friendship throughout her childhood.

The celebration of marriage, a growing family, and a community of friends, all are part of Dan, Mickie, Deirdre, and Renny's future.

Sounding the Gender-Bias Alarm

Some members of the legal community are sounding the alarm, New York Family Court Judy Sheindlin, in her book,

Don't Pee On My Leg and Tell Me It's Raining, boldly states her observations.

> "For the past twenty years we have encouraged men to become involved with their children from conception and Lamaze through birthing, feeding, diapering and quality time. We have fooled them into believing that the law means what it says, when it promises that fathers and mothers are treated equally in our courts....

> "American fathers are led down a primrose path every day in our family courts, often with disastrous legal results. They wind up in the Land of Gender Bias, where they are systematically stripped of their rights, often without the slightest idea of why it is happening to them."

Across the U.S.A. a grass-roots movement is growing. People are asking for an equitable, compassionate, non-adversarial system of divorce built on shared custody. Parents who have fought in the courts for the right to co-parent their own children are organizing and lobbying for laws that ensure the rights of fathers. Second wives, after seeing the suffering their husbands endure when dads are reduced to visitors, are assisting at all levels. Many people are witnessing the damage divorce is doing to children and as a result organizations devoted to children's rights are being supported federally and locally. Those in the counseling community are pointing out that attorneys are not trained to decipher what is in the children's best interest. Many family law judges agree that children's issues are better handled by counselors working directly with the moms and dads. And there are those too, in the medical professions, doctors, nurses, crisis center workers, who see the domestic violence that is often a by product of adversarial litigated divorces.

Most important of all, gender bias is motivating fathers to join together. The organizations vary in size and approach. Both federally and locally, fathers are opposing sole custody and promoting shared parenting. Some dads are patient, like those in the parenting focused peer support groups; they believe that social adjustments and changes in families are easier to accept when done slowly. Other organizations are more assertive: they want equality between parents, legally, socially, immediately. This is an exciting moment.

Poll Shows Most People Believe in Shared Parenting

A 1998, *U.S.A. Today* poll illustrates that most people believe in shared parenting:

The article "Fathers Wrestle for Their Rights" (May 30 - June 1, 1997) examined the rights of divorced dads in custody issues. Readers were asked for their opinions on which divorced parent generally should get custody of the kids.

Nearly 13,000 voted by calling an "800" number, by postcard or on-line. The question was "In custody battles where both parents are fit, what is best for the child?" The answers were:

- Mother gets custody: 13%

- Father gets custody: 13%

- Joint custody: 74%"

The fathers who supersede custody conflicts with shared parenting relationships by their actions send strong messages. People see them working hard to improve their position within the family. Such men believe in themselves as parents and know that they are an asset to their children. Communities are realizing that devoted fathers are a benefit to all. By their actions these parents disprove the negative stereotypes of men portrayed daily in the media. When the public views dads as intelligent, caring, contributing individuals that the community's children need to develop into healthy adults, then gender bias in the courts will end and fathers can be awarded the same privileges mothers receive.

New Organizations to Support Fatherhood

Fathers are showing the world that they are serious about shared parenting. Divorced dads, especially those practicing shared parenting, are beginning to help others to remain in their children's lives. People are noticing their involvement and attitudes about divorced men are changing. New organizations that support fatherhood are forming in cities across the U.S.A. Groups built on the idea of peer support are being founded to assist the thousands of newly divorced fathers who find themselves and their families in crisis each year.

There may be such an organization in your town. If not, there are sure to be single fathers eager to meet with men like themselves. More and more, groups of dads are meeting regularly to discuss how to improve the condition of their families. At these friendly and informal gatherings fathers are learning how to remain involved parents. Men are encouraged not to focus on what their ex-wives are doing; instead, fathers are learning the skills necessary to be the best of co-parents. In the company of such peers men newly divorced get a reprieve from worry. Their imaginations are fired and life takes on greater meaning. For an hour each week they can sit among friends and enjoy a fellowship built around a noble cause — sustaining the wellbeing of each other's families. No longer must a man sit alone and ponder what to do about child custody. Today, at the very least, there is peer support through the Internet; http://www.divorcedfathers.com will take you to a website where you can find support.

How to Start a Divorced Fathers' Network

Those who live in communities where meetings do not exist may want to start groups of their own. The first thing needed is a text. *Fathers Are Forever* is often used for the teaching of shared parenting. In a group setting the information within its chapters can be used for topics of discussion. Mothers and fathers can limit their exposure to conflict by following the suggestions printed on these pages. Because shared parenting is a long process and opportunities for misunderstandings do occur during the years it takes to raise children, most parents choose to keep *Fathers Are Forever* for future reference.

186

When starting a group it is helpful to have a copy of *Starting A Divorced Fathers Network*, by Steve Ashley. It can be purchased on the Internet at http://www.divorcedfathers.com. The booklet explains how to run the meetings, network within one's community, and how to sustain the group as it grows.

There are tremendous benefits to reaching out to the fathers in your community. When I was struggling in the early days of my family's breakup, a wise gentleman suggested to me that I stood to gain more from speaking with men going through divorce than I possibly could from relying on people like himself, far removed from the resources and process of divorce. His words rang true. I believe his advice saved my relationship with my daughter and possibly even my life. A fellow named Tom was the first divorced father I spoke with, thirteen years ago. He too was alone and suffering through visits with his children one afternoon a week. Tom understood completely how painful it was for me to be separated from my daughter. I looked forward to our meetings and always felt better after our conversations. We compared the gains and losses we experienced in our quests to create shared parenting. I owe much of my success at co-parenting to the fathers who have talked with me.

For the past twelve years Nancy and I have cooperatively raised Stephany. Today, our lives are far removed from the nightmarish days when she and I first parted ways. Stephany was a toddler then; today, she is fifteen — as healthy an individual as one will ever meet. After 15 years of shared experiences, both painful and joyous, my relationship with Nancy can best be described as a blend of respect and friendship. For us the drama of the past is inconsequential. To date, we have raised a healthy child. Still, there are pressing issues to contend with. It is a big job to fulfill the needs of a teenager, especially when she is juggling family and friends. Nancy and Stephany still ride horses. My daughter and I recently returned from a theater tour in London and Paris. Like many children, Stephany acts in high school plays. Her performances are a bright spot in both Nancy's and my live.

When it is curtain call and Stephany looks out at the audience she is sure to see her parents and their friends applauding, I know this is important to all in her family. When I look back at my experience of shared parenting and its benefits for my daughter, I am more devoted than ever to the idea of shared parenting.

I have committed myself to the purpose of helping divorced fathers fulfill their need to parent. As a result, each week I enjoy the company of men who like myself feel there is nothing more important than their roles as fathers. New dads attending our gatherings find a fellowship of men sharing laughter and compassion. Our meetings are inspiring; we know that the work we do benefits those involved. Lives are saved, relationships are altered for the better, and harmony is restored to families. When dads become versed in shared parenting, some in time move on and become leaders, founding groups in other cities, thus the network of fathers and the idea of shared parenting grows. There are few relationships that mean more to me than the ones I form with devoted dads. I look forward to the years of parenting that remain; there are three left before Stephany leaves home for college. I am committed to making the most of them.

To ensure that tomorrow's dads have every chance to raise their own children, today's fathers need to pass on to them the skills necessary to co-parent. Self-control during trying times, proficiency in learning parenting and communication skills, and the unwavering commitment to their children, these are the traits co-parents model. By our actions we can guarantee that the next generation of fathers will have every opportunity to nurture their children.

APPENDIX[*]

Co-Parenting and Virtual Visitation

Most everyone has seen a science-fiction movie that shows a parent communicating using a "video call" to talk with his or her children. The astronauts from the Apollo space program did this in the 1960's just as we saw it in the movie Star Trek. In the 80's we had Star Wars, in the 90's we saw

---

[*] **Contribution by Michael Gough,** author of *The Virtual Visitation Handbook - A Guide to Personal Video Conferencing.* COPYRIGHT © 2004-2006 INTERNETVISITATION.ORG

"video calling" in many movies and television shows depicting the future.

The future is here! Today, we can use video calling to stay in touch with our children. We can do so whether they are around the corner, across town, or across the country.

Virtual Visitation has many names: Virtual Parent-Time, Internet Visitation, Video Phone, Video Call, Computer Visitation, and others. The common legal term is "Virtual Visitation," which we will use here, though it may vary from state to state or individual preference. It involves using tools such as personal video conferencing, a webcam, email, instant messaging (IM) and other wired or wireless technologies.

Virtual Visitation is appropriate for:

- Divorced parents wanting to communicate with their children *and* one another
- Parents traveling on business or vacation wanting to keep in touch with other family members
- Grandparents wanting to communicate with distant family members, children and grandchildren
- Children whose parents are overseas on military assignment
- Counseling Centers facilitating parent-to-children communication
- Supervised visits for parents and their children
- Domestic violence and high conflict situations
- Parents and teachers seeking an inexpensive tool for remote education

What it is **NOT**: A replacement or substitute for in-person contact with one's children. Some have expressed concerns that Virtual Visitation is intended to substitute in-person or face-to-face visits with one's children. Not so. The most important contact you can have with your children is one-on-one, face-to-face. But, Virtual Visitation is a significant improvement over the telephone.

Most informed men support legislation that will protect parents' rights and guide the courts as to the proper use of this technology. That is, to "supplement" in-person visits, NOT to replace them.

Because I use Virtual Visitation when I travel, I'm now able to show my daughter cities all over the world, locations I could never describe over the phone. We read stories, learn typing, tell each other tales of the day and just plain connect.

Virtual Visitation also enables parents to confer more easily and for one parent to reinforce the decision of another. It can be used to visit with extended family members and, at the same time, help children feel they have two devoted and loving families even though their parents are divorced and living in separate homes.

My experience led me to crusade with the help of my Utah attorney, Joyce Maughan, to create the first bill, named in honor of my daughter, "Saige's Law" to add Virtual Visitation Amendments to the Utah divorce code, where it is now in effect. A Wisconsin law, "Electronic Communication," has also been passed. Our efforts have led to legislation being considered in many other states, from California to Maine.

The goal of the legislation is to educate the courts and attorneys, who will, in turn, inform all concerned as to the benefits and just uses of Virtual Visitation.

Adding Virtual Visitation to Your Divorce Settlement

Introduction

Disclaimer — I am not an attorney. Please consult legal counsel for any matters discussed in this chapter before making a decision.

Trends

Courts are increasingly implementing Virtual Visitation in child-related cases, recognizing children's critical need to have both parents in their lives. Judges will not be able to ignore the new technology as they weigh conflicting pleas from divorced parents. Advocates of Virtual Visitation say communicating over the Internet is especially helpful in cases that involve supervised visits. It is also being used as a remedy for non-custodial parents to remain in contact with their children. Moreover, laws are being passed to implement Virtual Visitation as an automatic option, like the telephone.

Step One

The first step in getting Virtual Visitation into your divorce settlement is to know what is required and the approximate costs — $800 in 2006 — associated with buying the equipment. See "Equipment Required" on next page.

Because this is a fairly new trend, you will probably need to have wording inserted into your divorce decree.

Note: For most current information on equipment and software, please check *www.InternetVisitation.org* and www.videocalltips.com. "The Virtual Visitation Handbook," available at *www.InternetVisitation.org*, is updated as new hardware and software becomes available.

Recommendation

Offer up the equipment as part of your divorce settlement. Doing so may prove cheaper than litigating over $800. You might then be in a position to negotiate for the ongoing Internet charges.

Wording for your Divorce Decree

Your legal counsel or attorney will help you adjust the wording to fit your specific state and situation.

Cooperative Relationship

For a cooperative relationship, a general order can suffice, such as, "The parties will cooperate to provide Virtual Visitation for the child with each parent."

High-Conflict Relationship

In high-conflict relationships, a tightly crafted order, with concrete specifications for implementation, can help make video conferencing a reality for the child.

Points to include in the order:

1. Which technologies are being ordered (video conferencing, email, instant messaging, cell phone, video cell phone, etc.)?

2. Equipment Required:
   - PC or Apple computer
   - Reliable webcam
   - Headset/microphone
   - Video and Voice software
   - High-Speed Internet (Cable/DSL) connection
     Note: In rural areas, a high-speed Internet connection may not be available. Speeds through satellite connections are not yet adequate (2006).
   - DSL/Cable Broadband router (for security)
   - Personal Firewall software (for security)
   - Virus and Spyware Protection (PCs)

3. Installation and training services if needed.

4. Which parent is required to pay for necessary equipment and services?
   That is, who will provide and pay for?
   - The needed equipment for the custodial parent?
   - The needed equipment for the non-custodial parent?
   - The monthly high-speed Internet connection for the custodial parent?

- The monthly high-speed Internet connection for the non-custodial parent?

5. Schedule, e.g., days of the week, number of times per week, and times of day for Virtual Visitation to occur (we recommend an hour or so before bedtime for young children).

6. Which parent is responsible for initiating the Virtual Visitation session?

7. Deadline for custodial parent to have equipment ready and video conferencing in full operation.

8. If equipment malfunctions, what time period is allowed for computer repair before court sanctions are triggered?

9. Remedies and sanctions for noncompliance, including contempt and attorney fees?

See examples below of divorce decree wording to review with your legal counsel:

Sample Divorce Decree Wording #1

Virtual Parent-Time and Telephone Time:

1. As provided by STATE CODE § XX-X-XX, and §XX-X-XX.X, telephone contact between the non-custodial parent and the Minor Child shall be at reasonable hours and for reasonable duration.

2. Both parents shall have voice mail or other means of taking telephone messages, so that the parent with whom the Minor Child is not residing may leave a message when they call the Minor Child. Both parents will cooperate to have the Minor Child return a call from the other parent as soon as possible. If a dispute arises about the number of calls, the parent with whom the Minor Child is not residing shall be entitled to no less than three telephone calls per week, including video conferencing. The Minor Child may contact either parent at any time the Minor Child wishes to do so, and the parent with the Minor Child will cooperate to help the Minor Child place the call.

3. Mother and Father shall each provide a computer and the following equipment in their own homes and keep it in working order for video conference parent-time with the Minor Child, and provide their user names and IP addresses (like a telephone number for the computer to be used) and any other necessary information, such as computer speed and network speed, to implement video conferencing:

3.1. 128K Internet speed minimum (upload and download)

3.2. Videoconference camera (webcam)

3.3. Software of quality equal to or better than MSN Messenger and Skype

3.4. Headset with microphone

3.5. Video card and monitor capable of resolution no lower than 1024 x 768

3.6. Full-Duplex Audio card

4. The parent where the Minor Child is not residing shall have the right to have virtual parent-time with the Minor Child through video conferencing on Sundays from 7:00 p.m. - 8:00 p.m. in the time zone where the Minor Child is. The parent in the home where the Minor Child is will cooperate to turn the computer on and off and help the Minor Child get set up for the video conference call so that things will be ready to go by 7:00 p.m. Other virtual parent-time shall be in accordance with the STATE CODE.

5. In addition, the Minor Child and the parent with whom the Minor Child is not residing may have video conference and telephone time with each other at reasonable times, and the parent who is with the child shall cooperate to place telephone calls and connect the video equipment.

6. When the Minor Child is out of town and unable to be at the video conferencing equipment, the schedule for video conferencing shall apply for telephone calls.

Sample Divorce Decree Wording #2

Telephone, E-Mail, and Video Conferencing with the Child —
Parental Communication Regarding the Child.

Each party may make reasonable telephone, e-mail, or video conferencing contact with the child while the child is at the home of the other party, during reasonable hours (determined by the location where the child is then located), for so long as such contact is not disruptive to the child's schedule. To facilitate such contact with the child, each party agrees to keep the other advised of all current home addresses and telephone numbers, including each party's cellular number(s), e-mail addresses, and other addresses at which electronic contact may be made, and to advise the other within forty-eight (48) hours of whenever a change in the same may occur. Each party agrees that it is in the best interests of the child for the parents to share information concerning the child. The petitioner shall provide an appropriate computer and service plan to be delivered to respondent's residence prior to the child's leaving for _____ with petitioner. Thereafter, the petitioner shall be fully and completely responsible for payment of all costs and expenses for necessary and desirable upgrades or replacements to the same, and shall provide ongoing payment to the respondent for monthly DSL or greater quality bandwidth and Internet service for two years. The petitioner shall, at all times, maintain a website for the child, with the same to include all current schedules, activities, pictures, and information regarding the child, and shall, at all times, ensure that the respondent, and respondent's family have complete access to the same. Respondent's privacy shall be deemed of paramount concern, and the petitioner hereby agrees that neither he, nor any third person or entity acting by his direction or on his behalf shall, in any way, monitor computer or electronic communication activities or communications of the respondent, either as the same occur with the child, or with any other person or entity.

Preparing for Court

In the unfortunate case that you have to go to court to request Virtual Visitation, you must be prepared to convince the court that Virtual Visitation is valuable. Hopefully, you will not have to show a demonstration in court, but if you do, then this section will give you an idea of what is needed and how to prove to the court that Virtual Visitation is easy to set up and inexpensive to use.

Getting Started

Your legal counsel will help decide the proper approach, but three areas need to be covered:

- What you actually want
- Supporting documentation
- A demonstration

How You Want to Set It Up

Your counsel will assist you with the items that are appropriate to your case. For example:

1. How many times per week do you want to perform Virtual Visitation? This will depend on the age of the children. The older they are, the more they can initiate conferencing without inconveniencing the custodial parent.

2. What days of the week will conferencing will take place?

3. What will be the time of day for your calls?

4. What is the duration of the calls you expect to make?

5. Who will provide and pay for the computer or dedicated Videophone device?

6. Who will provide and pay for the additional equipment (webcam and headset/microphone)?

7. Who will provide and pay for any required upgrades?

8. Who will provide and pay for the high-speed Internet connection?

You need to have a plan to address these questions before going to court. Be prepared to pay for all of it if you truly want video conferencing. Your counsel can assist in guiding you on how each of your incomes come into play.

Demonstration in Court

If you feel a detailed plan of what you want and supporting documentation are not enough, then a courtroom demonstration may be required.

You will not need any Internet, network connections or AC power as laptops have batteries and the additional equipment draws power from the laptops. Here is what you will need to perform a demonstration:

- Two laptops with network cards
- Two webcams
- Two combination headset/microphones
- A 25-foot Ethernet cable
- A short cross-over cable
- An Ethernet female-to-female connector (to connect the 25' Ethernet cable and cross-over cable)
- Microsoft NetMeeting and/or Microsoft Portrait These do not require connecting to the Internet to work.

You can rent laptops if necessary. The other components are inexpensive and, in any case, will be required once you start using Virtual Visitation.

Procedure for demonstration

1. Fully charge both laptops.

2. Connect the two laptops together using the two Ethernet cables with the connector and configure the IP addresses (e.g. 192.168.1.1 & 192.168.1.2).

3. Set up one laptop on the Judge's bench and the other by your chair.

4. Have a knowledgeable friend run one laptop while you show the Judge how easy it is to use video conferencing.

5. PRACTICE - PRACTICE - PRACTICE!!!

If you have a high-conflict situation you will need to know what computer the other parent has, if one exists, so that you can understand the configuration if there are issues with performance or functionality.

Be sure to ask for the following:

- Speed of the other parent's computer.

- How much RAM is in the computer?

- What type and how fast is the person's high-speed connection?

- What audio card is in the computer?

- A requirement to keep the computer current with patches and updated software versions.

Supporting Documentation

One of the more important things to provide the court is your exhibit. If your state resembles Utah, which had no Virtual Visitation cases tried at the Appellate Court or State Supreme Court level, then the court has nothing on which to base its decision except the information you provide. Ask your legal counsel for individuals who have been involved in Virtual Visitation cases in your state.

Additional Points that Support Video Conferencing

- "Preschool children often assume they are to blame for the divorce, relating it to some behavior on their part, such as making too much noise." Ruth Stirtzinger & Lorraine Cholvat, *The Family Home as Attachment for Preschool Age*, quoted in Gindes, Marion, *The Psychological Effects of Relocation for Children of Divorce*, 15 J. Divorce & Remarriage 105 (1991), "Journal of the American Academy of Matrimonial Lawyers," Vol. 15, 1998, p. 139.

- Restore broken relationships: In high-conflict situations, Virtual Visitation can allow a relationship to develop long distance when there was little or no relationship before between the child and the non-custodial parent. Shefts, Kimberly R., Virtual Visitation: *The Next Generation of Options for Parent-Child Communication,* "Family Law Quarterly,"Vol. 36, No. 2 (Summer 2002), p. 322.

- Child Support: There may be a direct correlation between increased involvement in their child's life and the non-custodial parent's willingness to pay child support. Shefts, p. 312, notes 46 and 47.

Broadband – Internet Connection

The primary goal of selecting a high-speed Internet provider is to get an upload speed of at least 150kbps, preferably 200kbps or faster. If you can get cable television, then most likely you can get a high-speed cable modem from your cable provider. High-speed Internet from your cable provider is the fastest option available for the home user. If you cannot get cable, then ask other high-speed Internet providers what their "minimum guaranteed" speed is.

Note: For most current information on equipment and software, please check *www.InternetVisitation.org* and www.videocalltips.com.

Recommendation: Cable modem

Broadband Router

A broadband router allows you to connect more than one computer to your high-speed connection or use Wireless (WiFi) within your home. A broadband router also provides a very good level of security to protect your system from malicious computer activity. Always consider a wireless version for your DSL/Cable router so you have flexibility in using your computer anywhere in your home. We recommend getting a router with 4 or more ports and 802.11g Wireless.

Recommended: Wireless 802.11g DSL/Cable router

Computer or No Computer

If one of the following reasons to get a dedicated videophone device is applicable in your situation, then select a dedicated video telephone device like the D-Link i2eye Videophone. Reasons for a dedicated Videophone device:

- Cost – you need the least expensive solution and do not have a computer.

- You are using it for family members who are not comfortable using a computer.

- You are using it in an elderly care facility.

- You are in a divorce situation with children under 5 who are not yet computer-savvy and cooperation is an issue with the other parent.

Otherwise a Macintosh or Windows PC will meet your needs. If you do not already own or want a Mac, then choose a computer running Windows.

Recommended: Computer running Windows XP

Intel-Based PCs

Many more options are available for the PC than the Mac and most people you will communicate with will have a PC.

Apple - Mac

If you already own a Mac or know you want to use a Mac on both sides, please take into account that AOL Instant Messenger (AIM Triton) supports communicating with Apple's iChat Audio Video (AV) solution. Some solutions apply to both PC and Mac versions, SightSpeed for example.

Which Mac?

If you have a Mac, anything later than an Apple G3 should work fine.

Apple's MacBook Pro, released in 2006, comes with a built-in iSight camera and iChat AV software. Apple's spiel says it all: "Just because you're a thousand miles away, there's no reason you can't attend the weekly staff meeting or read a bedtime story to your daughter. Not if you're traveling with a new MacBook Pro. With its built-in iSight camera and stellar iChat AV software, it provides everything you need to be face-to-face with family, friends, colleagues, or clients in just a few minutes."

PC Webcam

Many webcams will work. The top choices:

- Logitech QuickCam Pro 5000
- Logitech QuickCam for notebooks Pro (newer version)

Recommendation: Logitech QuickCam

Webcams for the Mac

- Apple iSight
- Logitech QuickCam Pro 4000
- Logitech QuickCam for Notebooks Pro (older version)

Recommendation: Apple iSight

Headset/Microphone

A combination Headset/Microphone is the same for either the PC or Mac. In making your decision, consider:

- How it fits
- What it costs

Use a headset/microphone designed to plug into your computer's audio card. They have two 1/8" plugs, one pink (microphone) and one green (headphone) connector. The following headset/microphone manufacturers are among the best:

- Plantronics
- Altec Lansing
- Logitech

You may also use your computer speakers with a noise-canceling microphone instead of a headset for a hands-free experience. Be sure to turn the volume down on the speakers when you are making a Video Call so the other side does not encounter echo or unwanted feedback.

Recommendation: Headset or Speaker and Microphone Combination

Personal Video Conferencing Solutions for the PC

Select one of the free solutions to start. Later you can evaluate other options depending on your needs.

- Microsoft MSN Messenger for video and Skype for audio
- Skype with Video4IM
- SightSpeed

The combination of MSN Messenger and Skype offers the best combination of video and audio. Skype has superb audio quality so using it with MSN is a complementary solution. Skype with a video plug-in, called Video4IM, is also a good solution.

Personal Video Conferencing Solution for the Macintosh

As with the PC, select one of the free solutions to start and evaluate others depending on your needs.

- SightSpeed (Windows and Macintosh)
- Apple iChat AV (Free with Mac OS X – Panther or later)
- AOL AIM Triton for Windows to users on a Mac using iChat AV
- Apple iChat AV also works with AIM Triton to give Apple iChat AV users the capability to chat with Windows users who cannot use iChat AV.

Recommendations: SightSpeed is the best overall solution for Windows to Mac Video Call. For Mac to Mac, choose either Apple's own iChat AV or SightSpeed.

Security and Privacy

Securing your Internet connection and your computer from malicious activity is essential. A DSL/Cable router or broadband router as they are also called is recommended in addition to personal firewall software.

Personal Firewall Software

In selecting a personal firewall solution consider what parental controls you might wish to invoke. Some features in a parental control solution may overlap with personal firewall features.

We recommend Symantec's Norton Internet Security Suite.

For Windows, an additional anti-spyware program is necessary.

For added security, all webcams come with a lens cover that you can use when the webcam is not in use. The lens can also be turned so it is not "looking" into the room or space.

Protecting Children from Internet Predators

Recently in a December *New York Times* article and on a January, 2006, Oprah show, child predators and pedophiles were discussed, showing the worst possible thing that could happen if a child is left to use a computer and the Internet unattended, the key term being "unattended."

Predators or pedophiles prey on children, in-person or using the Internet, to exploit them for a variety of reasons. These people present themselves to your children or find your children through chat rooms or personal websites like www.myspace.com, www.me.com and other personal information portals.

Children are placing information about themselves on the Internet to websites like www.myspace.com and www.me.com and many parents have no idea what their children are placing on such sites or what their children are actually doing on their computer at any given time.

Recently a school in Wisconsin went to www.myspace.com and collected information about their students and sent the information home to their parents. The information found shocked many and this has caused a lot of discussion to occur on the subject of "What is my child actually doing on the Internet?"

I am leading the effort at my daughter's school PTA on a Program of "Safe Surfing" and "Stranger Safety." I too am concerned and am taking action that I have learned through my career to help other parents do the same, provide information to help protect our children.

In my business of computer security, a common saying is "Trust but Verify." In computer security this is more than a saying, it is a driving force behind how we do our line of work. Our children should be no different. If you have approved your child using the Internet, you should also accept the parental responsibility to monitor your child's Internet activity. I have been asked a lot recently, "What can I do to protect my child?"

Of course, we support using webcams for Virtual Visitation. Adding a webcam to your computer does not add any additional risk to you or your children. The risk is un-monitored activity. Most webcam vendors have lens covers and you can always turn the webcam sideways, away from the living space when not in use, or even unplug it and put it away. This is very easy parenting that I call "Parenting 101."

Can you think of a better use for a computer than to communicate with your parents, family or friends, and on the case of Virtual Visitation, a child with their non-custodial parent? Of course when your children are not using the computer for Virtual Visitation with their non-custodial parent, the child could be doing just about anything with the equipment.

On the Oprah show, the basic suggestion was "unplug the webcam." This may be good in theory, but not practical for an ever-increasing Internet savvy society and those wanting or needing to use Virtual Visitation as a tool to help children stay close to both their parents after divorce. Practice "Parenting 101" and there is no risk and that is what these articles we provide will help you do.

Some simple advice: "If you connect your computer to the Internet and let your children use it, you as a parent have an obligation to monitor their activity." Again, good in theory, but we all know that we cannot watch our children's Internet activity 24x7... or can we ? (Answer: Yes we can.)

Please see http://www.internetvisitation.org for more information on how to protect your computer and how to protect your children from predators and pedophiles as they use the Internet and practice Virtual Visitation. You can learn how to monitor your children's Internet access and help teach or guide them how to surf the Internet safely. As good as the *New York Times* and Oprah show were to show you how scary things can be, they failed to tell you there are ways to reduce or virtually eliminate these risks.

We also want people to know that with the recommendations we make, you can solve the argument that webcams are bad things. It is up to you, the parent, to monitor your children's computer and Internet use to be sure they do not fall prey to the scary things that can happen, just as you must in everyday life. Monitor your children's Internet access with the information we provided and you can sleep at night knowing your children are using the Internet for learning and communication and avoiding the issues we have discussed.

Please contact www.InternetVisitation.org if you have any questions or need assistance with your case. We hope the information here helped you understand how to avoid the issues the Internet can bring to your children. For more information:

www.InternetVisitation.org

www.VideoCallTips.com

www.SkypeTips.com

TIPS FOR SUCCESSFUL VIDEO CONFERENCING

Lighting

Lighting is a crucial component for a successful video call. For optimal background color, conduct the video call under fluorescent lights. Direct sunlight is too bright and will wash out your face. Make sure your webcam faces away from an open window.

Look at the Webcam

During a desktop video conference, look straight at the computer monitor or the lens of the webcam.

Position SightSpeed's Video
Call Pop-Up Screen Underneath the Webcam

When SightSpeed is initiated, put the person in video call directly below the webcam. This will help your eyes stay near the lens of the webcam. (See SightSpeed, http://www.sightspeed.com.)

Clothing

Blue or dark green solid shirts are ideal. Try to avoid loud prints and stripes as well as black and white shirts since they absorb and reflect light making the wearer look pale.

Chair position

Sit in the middle of the chair. Because this is visual communication, posture is important. Try to sit straight, with your chair positioned in front of the webcam.

SUGGESTED READING

Ashley, Steve A. *Starting a Divorced Fathers Network.* Santa Cruz, California: Divorced Fathers Network, 2000.

Biller, Henry B. *Fathers and Families: Paternal Factors in Child Development.* Westport, Connecticut: Auburn House, 1993.

Blau, Melinda. *Families Apart: Ten Keys to Successful Co-parenting.* New York: G.P. Putnam's Sons, 1993.

Garrity, Carla B., and Mitchell A. Baris. *Caught in the Middle; Protecting the Children of High-Conflict Divorce.* New York: Lexington Books, 1994.

Johnson, Spencer. *The One Minute Father.* New York: William Morrow & Company, Inc., 1983.

Mackey, Wade C. *The American Father: Biocultural and Developmental Aspects.* New York: Plenum Press, 1996.

Ricci, Isolina. *Mom's House, Dad's House; Making Two Homes for Your Child.* New York: A Fireside Book, Simon & Schuster, 1997.

Ross, Julie A., and Judy Corcoran. *Joint Custody with a Jerk; Raising a Child with an Uncooperative Ex.* New York: St. Martin's Press, 1996.

NOTES